...mbers, Alexis Argüello, **HENRY ARMSTRONG**, ...nítez, Jimmy Bivins, Cecilia Braekhus, Charley ...eri, Ezzard Charles, Julio César Chávez, Billy ...ck Dempsey, Roberto Durán, Bob Fitzsimmons, ... Tyson Fury, Joe Gans, Arturo Gatti, Wilfredo ..., Regina Halmich, Naseem Hamed, Fighting ... **HOLYFIELD**, Bernard Hopkins, Naoya Inoue, ...ey Ketchel, Wladimir Klitschko, Jake LaMotta, ...RD, Lennox Lewis, Sonny Liston, Ricardo López, ...Y **MARCIANO**, Juan Manuel Márquez, Christy ...ern, Jimmy McLarnin, Carlos Monzón, Archie ..., Jack O'Brien, Rubén Olivares, Manuel Ortiz, ... Rijker, **SUGAR RAY ROBINSON**, Barney Ross, ... Saddler, Salvador Sánchez, Amanda Serrano, ..., John L. Sullivan, Johnny Ta..., ...aylor, ... Tszyu, Gene Tunney, **MIKE TYSON**, Oleksandr ...er, Jimmy Wilde, Ike Williams, Carlos Zárate

THE
100 GREATEST FIGHTERS

By Thomas Gerbasi

San Rafael • Los Angeles • London

CONTENTS

Introduction	4

Laila Ali	6
Muhammad Ali	8
Saúl Álvarez	12
Lou Ambers	14
Alexis Argüello	16
Henry Armstrong	18
Marco Antonio Barrera	20
Carmen Basilio	22
Wilfred Benítez	24
Jimmy Bivins	26
Cecilia Braekhus	28
Charley Burley	30
Joe Calzaghe	32
Miguel Canto	34
Tony Canzoneri	36
Ezzard Charles	38
Julio César Chávez	40
Billy Conn	42
Terence Crawford	44
Oscar De La Hoya	46
Jack Dempsey	48
Roberto Durán	50
Bob Fitzsimmons	52
George Foreman	54
Bob Foster	58
Joe Frazier	60
Tyson Fury	62
Joe Gans	64
Arturo Gatti	66
Wilfredo Gómez	68
Harry Greb	70
Emile Griffith	72
Marvelous Marvin Hagler	74
Regina Halmich	76
Naseem Hamed	78
Fighting Harada	80
Thomas Hearns	82
Larry Holmes	84
Evander Holyfield	86
Bernard Hopkins	88
Naoya Inoue	90
Éder Jofre	92
Jack Johnson	94
Roy Jones Jr.	98
Stanley Ketchel	100
Wladimir Klitschko	102
Jake LaMotta	104
Sam Langford	106
Benny Leonard	108
Sugar Ray Leonard	110
Lennox Lewis	112
Sonny Liston	114

Ricardo López	116
Tommy Loughran	118
Joe Louis	120
Ray Mancini	122
Rocky Marciano	124
Juan Manuel Márquez	128
Christy Martin	130
Floyd Mayweather Jr.	132
Terry McGovern	134
Jimmy McLarnin	136
Carlos Monzón	138
Archie Moore	140
Erik Morales	142
Shane Mosley	144
Azumah Nelson	146
Philadelphia Jack O'Brien	148
Rubén Olivares	150
Manuel Ortiz	152
Manny Pacquiao	154
Willie Pep	156
Aaron Pryor	158
Lucia Rijker	160
Sugar Ray Robinson	162
Barney Ross	166
Tommy Ryan	168
Matthew Saad Muhammad	170
Sandy Saddler	172
Salvador Sánchez	174
Amanda Serrano	176
Claressa Shields	178
Michael Spinks	180
Young Stribling	182
John L. Sullivan	184
Johnny Tapia	186
Katie Taylor	188
Dick Tiger	190
James Toney	192
Félix Trinidad	194
Kostya Tszyu	196
Gene Tunney	198
Mike Tyson	200
Oleksandr Usyk	202
Mickey Walker	204
Andre Ward	206
Pernell Whitaker	208
Jimmy Wilde	210
Ike Williams	212
Carlos Zárate	214
Greatest Fights	216
Greatest Knockouts	220
Best of a Nation	222

Introduction

THOMAS GERBASI

Muhammed Ali said he was "The Greatest," and I won't argue with him.

But many will, citing Sugar Ray Robinson, Henry Armstrong, Joe Louis, or any number of legends as the best boxer of all time.

I won't argue with them, either, because so many have a compelling case to make. And unlike sports such as baseball, football, basketball, hockey, and even soccer these days, the age of advanced analytics hasn't hit boxing yet.

Punch stats are recorded for major bouts, but they really don't mean much. After all, Fighter A can get outlanded 100 to 1 by Fighter B, but if that one punch landed knocks out the other fighter . . . well, you get the idea.

The point is, greatness is subjective in boxing. There's no number of home runs, baskets, touchdowns, or goals to match to get that recognition. A 20-0 record with twenty knockouts might look impressive, but not when the fighter with that perfect slate has been fighting lesser opposition. And some might scoff at a fighter losing a bout or two (or ten), but when the best fight the best, someone has to leave the ring without their hand raised, and that shouldn't be held against a superior athlete.

So what makes a boxer great? Talent helps, with grit and determination following closely behind. Domination of the era is also key, and fighting the best available opposition on a consistent basis truly sets the elite apart. But perhaps my favorite factor in determining greatness is impact. What boxers were you talking about at the water cooler at work the Monday after a fight? Who made you change your weekend plans so you could be in front of the TV or radio whenever they fought? And what fighters did your mother know, even though she wasn't a boxing fan?

If you ask a hundred people for their hundred greatest boxers, you might get a hundred different lists. This is mine. I've followed this sport since I was a kid, and I've been writing about it professionally for nearly three decades. That's a lot of fights and a lot of fighters. You might agree with my picks; you might not. There's really no right or wrong answer—we simply get to argue (civilly) and debate. At the very least, let's give all boxers their due.

Hugh McIlvanney described boxing as "The Hardest Game," and it's also the loneliest: No other sport reveals character quite like it, with two boxers trying to punch each other in the face while standing in a ring in their underwear. And when the final bell rings, finding something to replace that roar of the crowd is nearly impossible. Read about these fighters in the following pages, go look up their footage on YouTube, and appreciate what they gave to us.

I know I do. Here's my love letter to boxing. It's not a perfect sport, but when it's done right, there's nothing like it.

LAILA ALI

"SHE BEE STINGIN'"

LOS ANGELES, CA
BORN: December 30, 1977
HEIGHT: 5'10"
RECORD: 24–0 (21 KOs)
TITLES WON: World Super Middleweight Champion
HALL OF FAME INDUCTION: 2021

"A lot of times people see pictures of me in magazines and they see this pretty girl, and they don't realize that I'm really very street and I'm a fighter at heart," said Laila Ali. "So you're not going to get the smiley, 'I'm here to be cute' attitude. That's not me."

The greatest compliment we can pay to Ali is that she would have found her place onto this list of all-time greats even if she'd passed over her famous father's last name and fought under her mother Verónica's maiden name as Laila Porche.

But she did carry the name of her father, Muhammad Ali. As she entered the world of professional boxing she saw that last name as a gift, not a burden, despite accusations that she was doing it strictly for the fame and the money.

" think that people were skeptical in the beginning, but I expected that, and I knew that it would take time, no matter what anybody said."

Undeterred by the comments of critics, Ali put n the work in the gym. As her wins piled up, everyone saw that she wasn't a hype job: She was the real deal.

In her twelfth fight, Ali stopped Suzette Taylor in two rounds to become a world super middleweight champion. She went on to add more belts as the years passed, en route to a perfect 24–0 record, with twenty-one wins by knockout. Along the way, she brought attention to the sport that hadn't been there since the heyday of one of the fighters she'd beaten in 2003, Christy Martin. But whether or not you see Ali as a game changer, she's unconcerned. She's always been her own woman.

"I don't get into that conversation of, 'I wish I got my recognition,'" Ali said. "I did what I wanted to do, which was be a world champion, go undefeated, and be the best in my weight class. And that's all I can do. I didn't say I wanted people to call me the greatest female fighter of all time because I'm never gonna rely on what other people think for my happiness."

MUHAMMAD ALI

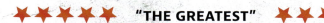 "THE GREATEST" ★★★★★

LOUISVILLE, KY
BORN: January 17, 1942
DIED: June 3, 2016
HEIGHT: 6′3″
RECORD: 56–5 (37 KOs)
TITLES WON: Three-Time World Heavyweight Champion; 1960 Olympic Gold Medalist
HALL OF FAME INDUCTION: 1990

Gallaghers Steakhouse in New York City was packed to the gills with media hoping to catch a glimpse of Muhammad Ali in 2002. Parkinson's disease had already started to take its toll on "The Greatest" when it came to Ali's speech and movement, but his mind and wit were as sharp as ever.

I was fairly new to the game, so I'd never gotten to cover the three-time heavyweight champion during his heyday—but now was my chance. I went to his longtime friend and photographer Howard Bingham and began to ask him a question to relay to Ali. "You can ask him yourself," said Bingham.

So I leaned over and asked Ali what it was like to still bring out a crowd like this after all these years. He turned to me and whispered in the most familiar voice in all of sports—and maybe the world:

"This crowd ain't big enough."

I still get chills telling that story, seeing Ali as vibrant and charismatic as ever, despite his body conspiring against him. That was the impact the man born Cassius Clay had on all of us. At one time in the 1970s, a poll was taken to determine the most recognizable person in the world—it was Ali, beating out Elvis Presley, Mao Tse-Tung, and Mickey Mouse for the honor.

Ali's story was the stuff of Hollywood screenwriter dreams, as if pulled right out of an epic film. He turned to boxing as a twelve-year-old after his bike was stolen because he was looking for revenge. He fell in love with the sport instead and went on to win an Olympic gold medal in 1960.

The pro game was the next logical step, and he didn't disappoint. Using speed, smarts, and an unorthodox style unlike anything anyone had seen before, he won the heavyweight championship for the first time in 1964 by beating the unbeatable Sonny Liston. And he got there by doing everything in the ring backward, purists said.

"I shook up the world," Ali proclaimed after the fight, and he continued to do just that. In 1967, he was stripped of his title and forced into a three-year exile for his courageous stand on the Vietnam War.

When Ali returned, he'd lost a step, but he was determined to prove his toughness. He took up three battles with Joe Frazier and won two of them. Then he toppled another seemingly invincible opponent in George Foreman. Ali's camp—and practically everyone else—feared for his safety when he traveled to Zaire to face "Big George." But the man who'd shaken up the world in 1964 did it again ten years later, knocking out Foreman in the eighth round to win the title for a second time.

Continuing to travel the globe as a world champion, Ali lost and regained the title once more in a two-fight series with Leon Spinks in 1978. He finally retired in 1981 as a true legend of the sport. Beyond boxing, though, Ali was a humanitarian, civil rights activist, and ambassador—not just for his sport, but also for life. He overcame incredible odds in and out of the ring, becoming an unforgettable figure in American history in the process.

On that day in New York City, he made it clear that he had no regrets.

"I'd do it exactly the same," said Ali. "Everything turned out perfect."

SAÚL ÁLVAREZ

 "CANELO"

GUADALAJARA, JALISCO, MEXICO
BORN: July 18, 1990
HEIGHT: 5'7½"
RECORD: 62–3–2 (39 KOs)*
TITLES WON: World Junior Middleweight Champion, World Middleweight Champion, World Super Middleweight Champion, World Light Heavyweight Champion

*As of press date

It's easy to forget this boxer's given name of Saúl Álvarez, despite his unforgettable status as the pay-per-view king of boxing with world titles in four weight classes. To his legion of fans, he's simply "Canelo."

Given that moniker because of his red hair, the Guadalajara native was born into boxing. All six of his older brothers donned the gloves at one time. By age thirteen, Álvarez was in the ring himself. From that point on, he never saw any other road for him to travel.

"I've always loved boxing, I've always been passionate about it, and it's something that I've always wanted to do," he said.

At the age of fifteen, Álvarez turned pro. Titles, big paydays, and worldwide superstardom followed in the next two decades, but his initial goals were simple.

"I respect the sport, and I would love for everybody in the sport to respect me," he told me in 2015. "I think that it's a very important thing for me. That's why I give my best—I want to be respected."

Álvarez especially wanted the respect of the discerning fight fans in his native Mexico. He earned that respect early on by taking on grueling challenges every step of the way and never lost it. Already 35–0–1 when he won his first title in 2011 by beating Matthew Hatton for the WBC junior middleweight belt, Álvarez added six more victories to his slate before facing unbeaten superstar Floyd Mayweather Jr. in 2013. He lost a majority decision that night, but the twenty-three-year-old learned valuable lessons and showed that he was very much a star in his own right.

He didn't lose again for nine years. During that unbeaten stretch, Álvarez posted wins over Miguel Cotto, Amir Khan, Gennadiy Golovkin, Daniel Jacobs, and Sergey Kovalev. Dmitry Bivol stopped that run in 2022, but then Álvarez started a new winning streak that stands at six as of May 2025.

LOU AMBERS

 "THE HERKIMER HURRICANE"

HERKIMER, NY
BORN: November 8, 1913
DIED: April 25, 1995
HEIGHT: 5'4½"
RECORD: 89–8–7, 2 NC (28 KOs)
TITLES WON: World Lightweight Champion
HALL OF FAME INDUCTION: 1992

Luigi Giuseppe d'Ambrosio wasn't afraid of anybody—except his mother. So when "The Herkimer Hurricane" decided he was going to become a boxer, he entered the ring under the name Lou Ambers so that his mom wouldn't find out.

Eventually, Mrs. d'Ambrosio saw her son become an elite prizefighter. After every fight, he even called to let her know he was all right.

Usually, he was able to tell her that he'd won, too—89 times in 104 bouts, to be exact. It was a remarkable slate, considering that he fought professionally only from 1932 to 1941; that's an average of 11½ fights a year, a number that dwarfs modern-era pugilists.

But those were different times, and fighters like Ambers were built different. Hungry to help his family during the Great Depression, Ambers reflected that hunger in the ring, mixing toughness with a volume punching attack that kept his foes off balance. That was quite a feat, considering who he battled during his career: a Murderers' Row that included Tony Canzoneri, Fritzie Zivic, Baby Arizmendi, Jimmy McLarnin, Henry Armstrong, and Lew Jenkins.

A lightweight champion from 1936 to 1938 and again from 1939 to 1940, Ambers retired after his 1941 loss to Jenkins. He served with the Coast Guard during World War II and lived a full life until his death in 1995 at the age of eighty-one.

ALEXIS ARGÜELLO

 "EL FLACO EXPLOSIVO"

MANAGUA, NICARAGUA
BORN: April 19, 1952
DIED: July 1, 2009
HEIGHT: 5'10"
RECORD: 77–8 (62 KOs)
TITLES WON: World Featherweight Champion, World Super Featherweight Champion, World Lightweight Champion
HALL OF FAME INDUCTION: 1992

It was storming in Nicaragua when my 1998 interview with Alexis Argüello abruptly got cut off. Writing was a part-time gig for me at the time, so I had to go to work the next day. I asked my wife to call Argüello, thank him for his time, and let him know that I got what I needed. He told her to have me call back that night: "We were just getting into some good stuff."

We talked again that night. This was before unlimited calling and international plans, so the interview cost me $130. It was worth every penny.

For everyone who saw "El Flaco Explosivo" on television and witnessed his public demeanor as one of boxing's great ambassadors, he was like that in private, too. That's rare in any walk of life, but especially in boxing, where fighters are expected to adopt dramatic, larger-than-life personas. Yet the native of Managua never forgot where he'd come from and how he'd been raised, even when entering the fistic shark tank.

"Actually, my influence was my needy situation," Argüello said. "I was poor. My father was a shoemaker. My mom used to sell shoes in the street. And I got thrown out of school because my father couldn't afford to pay. And you, I, and all human beings come to this world with a talent, with a goal. And when I was fifteen, I got something deep in my heart, something that I felt my country needed. There were three guys from my country who tried to win a world title, and they failed. And I went for the first time to the gym, and I liked it. As days went by, I kept thinking of the idea of being the first guy to win a world title for my country."

Argüello, a lanky boxer with dynamite in his gloves, hit his mark in his second try when he defeated Rubén Olivares for the WBA featherweight title in November 1974. It was one of three divisional titles the "Explosive Thin Man" won. The sport was aired on free network television in the 1980s, and Argüello

was a staple. His gentlemanly demeanor and action-packed style turned him into a star.

He may have been his best at 130 pounds, when he defeated Alfredo Escalera, Bazooka Limón, Bobby Chacon, and Ruben Castillo, but his lightweight run took him to new heights in terms of recognition. When he moved up even further to the junior welterweight division to face Aaron Pryor in 1982, he delivered a SuperFight that lived up to the hype, even if Pryor emerged victorious both in that first fight and in their 1983 rematch.

Surprisingly, after such a pair of violent battles, the two became friends and often ran into each other at boxing functions. "We never refer to our fights," Argüello said. "The only thing we feel is that we have a bond with each other, a common bond that pressures us to respect each other because we are in a brotherhood. We had two battles, and such a bond between us."

Considering Argüello's character, that's not surprising at all.

HENRY ARMSTRONG

★★★★★ "HOMICIDE HANK" ★★★★★

COLUMBUS, MS
BORN: December 12, 1912
DIED: October 22, 1988
HEIGHT: 5'5½"
RECORD: 149–21–10 (99 KOs)
TITLES WON: World Featherweight Champion, World Lightweight Champion, World Welterweight Champion
HALL OF FAME INDUCTION: 1990

Modern professional boxing has seventeen weight classes, with four "major" world titles in each division.

When Henry Armstrong fought in his heyday in the 1930s and '40s, there was one champion in each of eight weight classes. Armstrong once held three of those titles—simultaneously. It was a remarkable feat that has never been matched.

He nearly notched a fourth divisional title in 1940 when he challenged Ceferino Garcia for the middleweight crown. A draw that most observers believed should have been a win for Armstrong.

We can stop right there to show why Armstrong is a hall-of-famer and an all-time great. But names, numbers, and titles don't tell the whole story of "Homicide Hank." In fact, one nickname wasn't even enough for the Mississippi native: He also went by "Hurricane Hank" and "Hammerin' Hank."

Whatever he was called, promoters didn't have to look hard to find him. Armstrong was willing to fight anyone, anywhere, at any time. Granted, boxers of that era regularly kept busy and took on tough competition, but Armstrong took that attitude to new levels and fought with an intensity that wore down even the toughest opponents—if he didn't knock them out first.

Surprisingly, Armstrong lost his debut pro fight in July 1931 and started his career with a middling 1–3 record. Those early beginnings didn't predict the future, though—not by a long shot. The year 1937 is most often cited as his definitive display of excellence. During that year, he compiled a 27–0 slate that included twenty-six knockouts, highlighted by a sixth-round knockout of Petey Sarron that earned him the featherweight title.

In May 1938, he added the welterweight title by beating Barney Ross. Three months later, he took the lightweight title with a victory over Lou Ambers.

Armstrong was indeed the undisputed king of the boxing world.

MARCO ANTONIO BARRERA

 **"THE BABY-FACED ASSASSIN"**

MEXICO CITY, MEXICO
BORN: January 17, 1974
HEIGHT: 5'6"
RECORD: 67–7, 1 NC (44 KOs)
TITLES WON: World Champion at Junior Featherweight, Junior Lightweight, and Featherweight
HALL OF FAME INDUCTION: 2017

In the classic 1954 film *On the Waterfront*, Marlon Brando's character, Terry Malloy, famously says, "I coulda been a contender." Well, Mexican boxing great Marco Antonio Barrera could've been a lawyer. In fact, the Mexico City native was as deep into his studies at La Salle University as he was into his ring career when he decided that he needed to focus solely on hitting opponents, not the books.

Boxing won, and so did the fans who watched him ply his trade in some of the biggest fights of his era. Barrera didn't come from the typical hard-luck background so many fistic greats did, but he had talent and pride. When he stepped between the ropes, he didn't do it just for himself—he fought for Mexico.

"A Mexican believes that once you sign that contract, you go into that ring and leave it all there—your anger, your pride, everything," said Barrera. "And whether you win or lose, you can never come back and say that I should have done this, or I should have done that."

Barrera won his first forty-three pro fights and a world junior featherweight title before he lost to Junior Jones in 1996 and again during their 1997 rematch. Those losses, coupled with an epic war against Kennedy McKinney, made many critics wonder if Barrera was a shooting star about to fizzle out.

Enter Tijuana's Erik Morales. From 2000 to 2004, the pair engaged in a classic trilogy that will live on forever in the hearts of boxing fans who saw both fighters leave everything in the ring in search of victory.

"We did it out of a love for the sport," said Barrera. 'We wanted to hear that applause at the end of the fight."

They got it. In the process, Barrera resurrected his career. And whether it was thanks to his trilogy against "El Terrible" or his memorable bouts against Naseem Hamed, Johnny Tapia, Kevin Kelley, Juan Manuel Márquez, and Manny Pacquiao, it seems that the 2017 International Boxing Hall of Fame inductee made a good call in leaving school behind.

CARMEN BASILIO

 **"THE UPSTATE ONION FARMER"**

CANASTOTA, NY
BORN: April 2, 1927
DIED: November 7, 2012
HEIGHT: 5′6½″
RECORD: 56–16–7 (27 KOs)
TITLES WON: World Champion at Welterweight and Middleweight
HALL OF FAME INDUCTION: 1990

Before smartphones and social media made life a lot easier, a writer actually had to put in some work to get to a retired athlete, especially one as accomplished as Carmen Basilio.

So out came the pen and paper, and I wrote to "The Upstate Onion Farmer" at his home in New York (back then, you could buy a book with athletes' addresses in it so that you could ask for autographs). I wasn't expecting much, but, a couple weeks later, I received a letter with Basilio's autograph and phone number.

Unfortunately, we never got to speak, but I tell this story to show that, for all his accolades in the ring—which included an induction into the International Boxing Hall of Fame, in his hometown of Canastota—Basilio never let success get to his head. To the people he met, he was an everyman—albeit one with the otherworldly toughness and drive that made him a world champion at welterweight and middleweight.

Mind you, this wasn't an average time for fighters in those weight classes. When Basilio was making his way, those divisions held some of the most tough and talented boxers ever. Just look at some of the names Basilio fought: Sugar Ray Robinson, Gene Fullmer, Tony DeMarco, Kid Gavilán, and Ike Williams, just to name a few.

But as talented as that crew was, if any of them were in the ring with Basilio, they were in for a fight and the fans were in for a treat. For a record five years in a row, Basilio was involved in *The Ring* magazine's Fight of the Year with DeMarco, Johnny Saxton, Robinson (twice), and Fullmer.

This willingness to leave it all in the ring every night made Basilio a hero to legions of boxing fans, who were able to thank him every June when he made his trip to the hall of fame for induction weekend. "Thank you" was the least we could do.

WILFRED BENÍTEZ

★★★★★ "EL RADAR" ★★★★★

SAN JUAN, PUERTO RICO
BORN: September 12, 1958
HEIGHT: 5'10"
RECORD: 53–8–1 (31 KOs)
TITLES WON: World Champion at Junior Welterweight, Welterweight, and Junior Middleweight
HALL OF FAME INDUCTION: 1996

Like his contemporary Thomas Hearns, Wilfred Benítez exuded cool. For proof, just look at his long staredown with Sugar Ray Leonard before their 1979 fight, or the way he dropped his hands and smiled after scoring a one-punch knockout of Maurice Hope.

But style without substance means nothing, and the man dubbed both "El Radar" and "The Bible of Boxing" had more to offer than most. Sure, he had the physical gifts of speed and agility, but it was Benítez's fight IQ and ability to see two steps ahead of his opponent that made him special. And let's not forget that he won his first world title at the age of seventeen.

Yes, by seventeen, the teenage *wunderkind* from Puerto Rico had already established his pedigree on a second island—Manhattan—and boasted a 25–0 record. Yet when he got a shot at Antonio Cervantes in March 1976, few gave him a real chance of winning. Benítez had other ideas and took a close and competitive split decision over the Colombian star. The still-growing teen wasn't long for the junior welterweight division, though. By 1979, he was a two-division champ after defeating Carlos Palomino for the 147-pound belt.

How did he do it? Well, first, he was a master boxer. But Benítez wasn't afraid of getting into a brawl, either, and he had the power to earn his respect. Needless to say, when a fight with Leonard was signed, boxing fans around the globe tuned in because it wasn't just the two best welterweights in the world facing off: The fighters entered the ring with a combined record of 63–0–1, all at the ages of twenty-one (Benítez) and twenty-three (Leonard).

The fans weren't disappointed, even though Benítez surely was: He lost his title to Leonard via TKO in the fifteenth and final round, as the showman

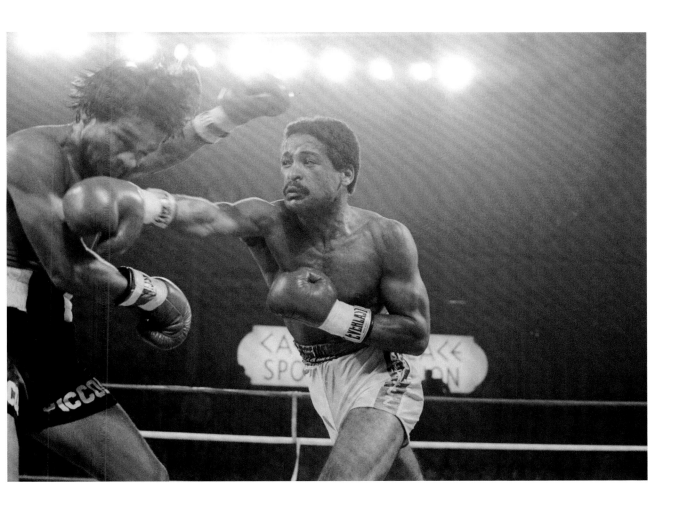

he was. But the Puerto Rican star rebounded quickly, stringing together a series of iconic battles: He won the junior middleweight title by knockout against Hope in 1981, took a decision win over Roberto Durán, and lost a close majority decision to Hearns.

These bouts against Leonard, Durán, and Hearns had many fans insisting that the unofficial "Four Kings" (which included Marvin Hagler) be renamed the "Five Kings," with the fifth crown going to Benítez.

The new moniker didn't catch on in the boxing mainstream, but for Benítez faithful, the Puerto Rican prodigy will always stand tall as the fifth king.

JIMMY BIVINS

CLEVELAND, OH

BORN: December 6, 1919
DIED: July 4, 2012
HEIGHT: 5'9"
RECORD: 86–25–1 (31 KOs)
TITLES WON: None
HALL OF FAME INDUCTION: 1999

They didn't write books about Jimmy Bivins, make films chronicling his life, or sing songs celebrating what he brought to the squared circle.

Maybe they should have.

Although the pride of Cleveland, Ohio, never received the opportunity to fight for a championship, when his name came up for induction into the International Boxing Hall of Fame in 1999, he received his rightful place among the greats.

But why didn't Bivins, owner of a career record of 86–25–1 (with thirty-one of those victories being knockouts) ever get his chance to shine on the sport's biggest stages? Most likely, he was just a little *too* good: With a stiff jab and defensive wizardry that baffled his foes, few could touch him when he was on top of his game.

A standout in three divisions, from middleweight to heavyweight, Bivins boasts a resume that includes wins over Charley Burley, Anton Christoforidis, Teddy Yarosz, Gus Lesnevich, Bob Pastor, Joey Maxim, Archie Moore, and Ezzard Charles.

In modern-day boxing, that list of wins would have earned Bivins at least a few world title shots, not to mention a championship, but it was not to be.

Bivins served briefly in World War II. When the war was over, he lost a step, falling to Charles, Moore, Jersey Joe Walcott, and Joe Louis. Impressively, Bivins fought fellow hall-of-famers Charles and Moore five times each, marking him as a unicorn of boxing. He also left the sport on a high note, running off four consecutive wins before he retired for good in 1955.

CECILIA BRAEKHUS

 "THE FIRST LADY"

BERGEN, NORWAY
BORN: September 28, 1981
HEIGHT: 5'7½"
RECORD: 38–2–1 (9 KOs)*
TITLES WON: World Champion at Welterweight,
Interim World Champion at Junior Middleweight

*As of press date

As Cecilia Braekhus approached her forty-third birthday in 2024, it's safe to say that she had earned a victory lap.

Undisputed welterweight champion from 2014 to 2020; the first woman in any weight class to hold four belts simultaneously; the first woman to fight on HBO; three recognitions from the Guinness Book of World Records; and the first recipient of the Boxing Writers Association of America's Christy Martin Award for best female boxer.

That's quite a resume. But ask "The First Lady" about her accomplishments, and she'll quickly deflect the praise onto others she opened the door for.

"I'm getting into the last years of my career, and I see all these girls blossoming, and I see big fights and they're making money, and I'm so incredibly happy that this is happening," said Braekhus. "I see they have an audience, they're getting the attention they deserve, and the conversation around the fights is about how they deserve to be here, and I'm so happy."

The women getting those legitimate paydays and worldwide exposure on big cards might not be in that position if not for Braekhus. A native of Colombia, Braekhus was adopted by Norwegian parents at the age of two and went on to become a superstar both in Norway and around the world.

Yet during her formative fighting years, there weren't opportunities for women like there are now, so after Braekhus won her first championship in 2009, she had to fight, fight, and fight some more to get the attention she deserved. Growing up in public as a young fighter, she learned to evolve her style: Her smooth technique and uncanny ability to avoid getting rattled rapidly cemented her place as a peerless boxer on a level of her own. In 2014, she became a three-belt champion by defeating Ivana Habazin, and the momentum only kept growing from there.

In 2016, Braekhus added another belt to her collection and began defeating the sport's best,

including Anne-Sophie Mathis, Erica Farias, and Kali Reis, with the Reis bout broadcast on the premium cable network HBO. She also played a pivotal role in getting professional boxing legalized in Norway after a thirty-three-year ban.

Although she lost the only two fights of her career to date to Jessica McCaskill in 2020 and 2021, the victory lap on her career will have to wait, considering that Brækhus celebrated her forty-third birthday a little early by defeating Maricela Cornejo for the interim junior middleweight title in August 2024. As for her ultimate goal, that's already a mission accomplished.

"I hope I will be remembered for opening some doors and shattering some glass ceilings and being a part of boxing history," Brækhus said. "That is my dream and my goal."

CHARLEY BURLEY

PITTSBURGH, PA
BORN: September 6, 1917
DIED: October 16, 1992
HEIGHT: 5'9"
RECORD: 83–12–2, 1 NC (50 KOs)
TITLES WON: None
HALL OF FAME INDUCTION: 1992

Charley Burley never won a world championship, but several of his peers—and even more fans and pundits—called him the greatest boxer to ever grace the ring.

That's high praise for the Pennsylvania native, but it's an even greater indictment of a system and society that held Burley back because of the color of his skin. There was even a name for the group of fighters like Burley who were avoided at all costs: Murderers' Row.

No less an authority than legendary trainer Eddie Futch described Burley as "the finest all-around fighter I ever saw," and he wasn't alone in that assessment. Racial oppression kept Burley from putting a world championship belt around his waist, but the welterweight and middleweight titleholder compiled a resume any boxer would envy.

A pro for fourteen years, from 1936 to 1950, Burley became an in-demand attraction at home in Pittsburgh, where local fans quickly found out that he could do it all in the ring. Whether boxing or banging, Burley either befuddled foes with his technique or halted them with his power. And if an opponent did land, it rarely affected the fighter: He was never stopped in ninety-eight bouts.

Soon enough, though, Burley realized that he wasn't going to be cut any breaks on the business side, so he had to control what he could—and that was what happened in the ring.

Owner of wins over Archie Moore, Fritzie Zivic, Billy Soose, and fellow Murderers' Row member Holman Williams, Burley was obviously world championship caliber, but no champion wanted to fight him. That forced him to find jobs as a sanitation worker and aircraft mechanic to make ends meet. Thankfully, the slights he endured during his career ended when he became a member of the International Boxing Hall of Fame.

JOE CALZAGHE

 "THE PRIDE OF WALES"

NEWBRIDGE, WALES
BORN: March 23, 1972
HEIGHT: 6'0"
RECORD: 46–0 (32 KOs)
TITLES WON: World Super Middleweight Champion
HALL OF FAME INDUCTION: 2014

Jeff Lacy was going to beat Joe Calzaghe. Despite Calzaghe's pristine 40–0 record and the fact that he had already successfully defended his WBO super middleweight title seventeen times (beating the likes of Chris Eubank, Robin Reid, Richie Woodhall, Charles Brewer, and Byron Mitchell along the way), many believed the Welshman wasn't going to be a match for the power-punching Olympian from the United States.

Then on March 4, 2006, the bell rang at the M.E.N. Arena in Manchester, and Calzaghe put on a clinic, dropping the undefeated Lacy and nearly shutting him out over twelve rounds.

"There is no easy way in fighting," said Lacy. "And one day, you're gonna meet that one person—Joe Calzaghe—who's gonna stand there and outmaneuver you and mentally and physically beat you in front of the world."

Europe already knew how good Calzaghe was, but now the rest of the world knew. And although the win over Lacy was a defining moment for "The Pride of Wales," it would not be the last: Calzaghe retired with a perfect 46–0 (thirty-two knockouts) record.

In fact, what defined Calzaghe's greatness wasn't the unbeaten slate, but rather how, when the fights continued to get bigger and more important, Calzaghe always lifted his game to reflect the high stakes involved. When Calzaghe closed his career with a trio of bouts against Mikkel Kessler, Bernard Hopkins, and Roy Jones Jr., he was at his best—fast, accurate, and more than willing to outwork his opponent.

This flawless body of work landed Calzaghe a well-deserved place in the International Boxing Hall of Fame.

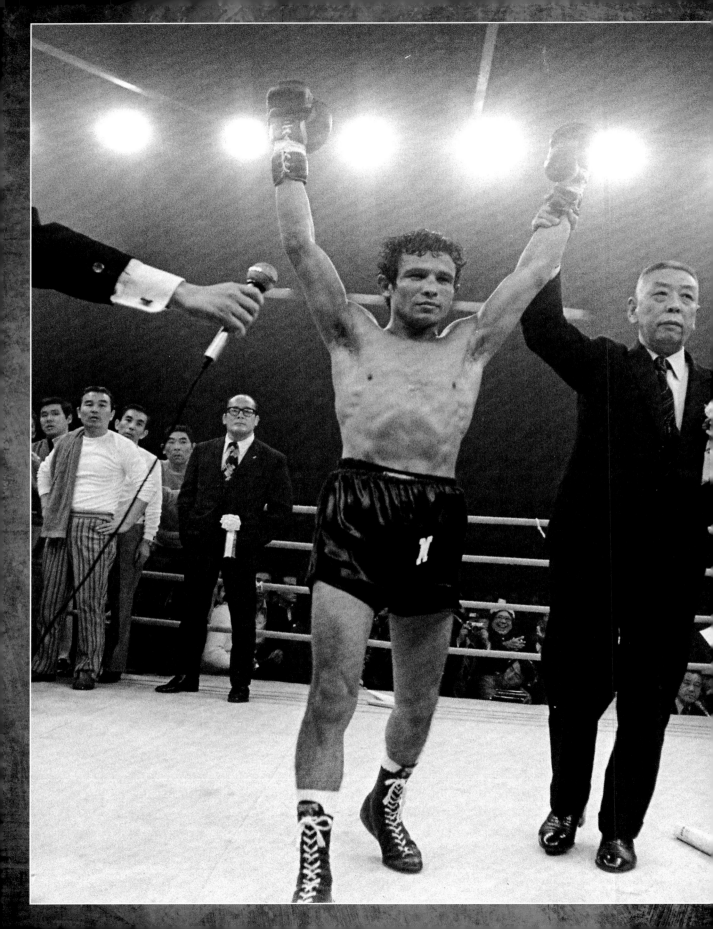

MIGUEL CANTO

★★★★★ "EL MAESTRO" ★★★★★

MÉRIDA, YUCATÁN, MEXICO
BORN: January 30, 1948
HEIGHT: 5'1½"
RECORD: 61–9–4 (15 KOs)
TITLES WON: World Flyweight Champion
HALL OF FAME INDUCTION: 1998

When Mexican fighters are brought up in boxing discussion, conversations usually center on the likes of Julio César Chávez, Rubén Olivares, and Erik Morales, usually in reverence to their pressure and power in the ring. Miguel Canto, on the other hand, earned his place among the greats for his technical boxing ability that earned him the nickname "El Maestro."

It's a fitting moniker for the native of Mérida, Yucatán, who was running a symphony in the ring when he was at the top of his game. It was subtle, it was sublime, and, for true aficionados of the sport, it was beautiful.

Shockingly, given where his career ultimately went, Canto lost his first pro bout via TKO to Raúl Hernández on February 5, 1969. Want another shocker? He dropped his third fight via TKO to Pedro Carillo, putting him at 1–2. For some fighters, that would be a career death sentence, but Canto was just getting warmed up: He went 32–1–3 over his next thirty-six fights, earning him a shot at Betulio González and the vacant WBC flyweight title in August 1973.

González left the ring with the belt via majority decision, but after six wins, Canto got another crack at the crown. This time, he won it, beating Shoji Oguma on January 8, 1975. No one touched Canto over the next four years, as he successfully defended his title fourteen times, beating González and Oguma two more times each along the way.

Canto was upset by Chan Hee Park in 1979 and lost his belt. Although he got a rematch, it ended in a draw, the closest he would get to reclaiming the championship. Canto retired after a 1982 loss to Rodolfo Ortega.

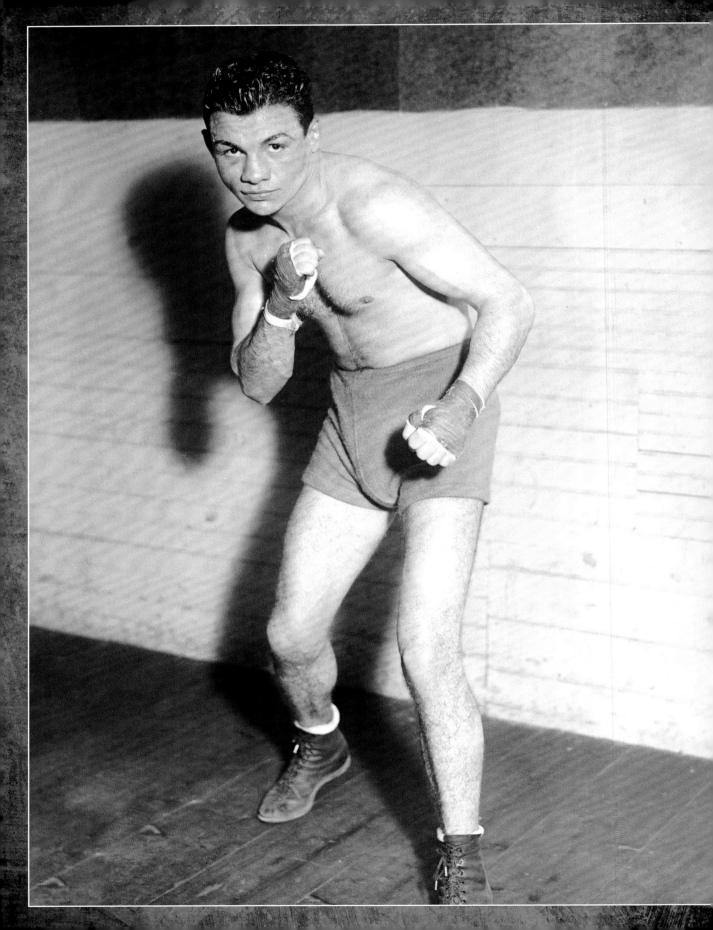

TONY CANZONERI

SLIDELL, LA
BORN: November 6, 1908
DIED: December 9, 1959
HEIGHT: 5'4"
RECORD: 137–24–10 (44 KOs)
TITLES WON: World Champion at Featherweight,
Lightweight, and Junior Welterweight
HALL OF FAME INDUCTION: 1990

My father always loved boxing. Although he didn't get to chase after his own dreams in the ring after a cut hand forced him out of the New York Golden Gloves, he didn't tire of telling his story of meeting Tony Canzoneri, who shook his hand and said, "How ya doin', kid?"

As the phrase goes, this is when giants walked among us. There was no army of handlers, no entourage, no barriers between a sporting superstar and the public. And make no mistake about it, Canzoneri was a superstar at the height of his powers in the 1920s and '30s as he won titles in three divisions. Today such a feat is almost routine, thanks to the proliferation of weight classes and sanctioning bodies. When Canzoneri pulled it off, though, it was rare.

Canzoneri started at bantamweight but ended his career at junior welterweight. He won 137 fights against only twenty-four losses and ten draws. A look at his record cements his place as an all-time great, thanks to victories over eighteen world champions. That who's who included Kid Chocolate, Jimmy McLarnin, Billy Petrolle, and Bud Taylor.

But Louisiana's Canzoneri is probably best remembered for his trilogy with fellow great Lou Ambers. Packing Madison Square Garden three times, the pair of evenly matched rivals slugged it out to the delight of their fans. Canzoneri won the first bout, and Ambers took the next two. But a series like that raises the stock of both fighters, regardless of the result. It was the perfect cornerstone to a career that garnered Canzoneri a legion of fans, including that aforementioned kid from Brooklyn.

EZZARD CHARLES

 "THE CINCINNATI COBRA"

CINCINNATI, OH
BORN: July 7, 1921
DIED: May 28, 1975
HEIGHT: 6'0"
RECORD: 95–25–1 (52 KOs)
TITLES WON: World Heavyweight Champion
HALL OF FAME INDUCTION: 1990

When it comes to underrated greats of the game, few have flown under the radar quite like Ezzard Charles. The reasons are baffling, because the body of work put together by "The Cincinnati Cobra" is matched by few.

Maybe being a heavyweight champion between Joe Louis and Rocky Marciano played a role in this, but the scary part about Charles's talent is that he might have already been past his prime when he defeated Jersey Joe Walcott for the title in June 1949. He went on to successfully defend his crown eight times, beating Louis and Walcott (again) before returning the title to Jersey Joe in 1951.

Charles got a chance to regain the title, engaging in a pair of bouts with new king Marciano in 1954. He lost both but still displayed enough flashes of his past brilliance to make the fights competitive. Charles fought only four years more, showing that perhaps his best years were when he dominated the middleweight and light heavyweight divisions.

He never won world titles at 160 and 175 pounds, but he beat Charley Burley, Teddy Yarosz, and Anton Christoforidis at middleweight before he moved to light heavyweight and continued his reign of excellence, scoring victories over Joey Maxim, Archie Moore, Lloyd Marshall, and Jimmy Bivins, among others.

To put a bow on everything, Charles fought International Boxing Hall of Fame members twenty-nine times and won twenty of those bouts. Needless to say, this true legend got the call to the hall's first class in 1990, fifteen years after his death at age fifty-three due to amyotrophic lateral sclerosis.

JULIO CÉSAR CHÁVEZ

★★★★★ "EL LEÓN DE CULIACÁN" ★★★★★

CULIACÁN, MEXICO
BORN: July 12, 1962
HEIGHT: 5'7½"
RECORD: 107–6–2 (85 KOs)
TITLES WON: World Champion at Junior Lightweight, Lightweight, and Junior Welterweight
HALL OF FAME INDUCTION: 2011

Mexico has produced a seemingly endless array of great fighters. But ask anyone who was the greatest, and you'll get only one answer: Julio César Chávez.

It's awfully tough to dispute. For most of his twenty-five-year career, "The Lion of Culiacán" was unstoppable, a relentless force whose pressure and body punching made some of the best fighters in the world wilt as he won world titles in three divisions. He wasn't flashy, but he was great—and he was loved.

"I always went and fought in the ring, giving my best, with only one goal: to win and give the best of me as a boxer," Chávez said. "As a boxer, you always know that you have your fans backing you up, and you wouldn't like to let them down."

He rarely did. Even when he was in jeopardy of seeing his 68–0 record turn to 68–1 against undefeated former Olympic gold medalist Meldrick Taylor in their 1990 SuperFight, he soldiered on: Before the twelfth and final round of the fight, he was losing on two of the three judges' scorecards, but he was determined to find a miracle.

"I really wanted that fight to end," Chávez admitted. "I was tired and thought I couldn't go anymore, but I really knew I had to give everything in me. That's how I am. In the last round of the fight with Meldrick Taylor, my corner told me to give everything, to do it for Mexico. And that's when I realized that the whole country was counting on me."

Chávez stopped Taylor with one second remaining in the fight, adding to a legend that continued to grow as he faced the best fighters of his era, including Héctor Camacho, Pernell Whitaker, Oscar De La Hoya, Frankie Randall, Tony Lopez, and Kostya Tszyu. When he retired in 2005, his status as a Mexican icon was secure.

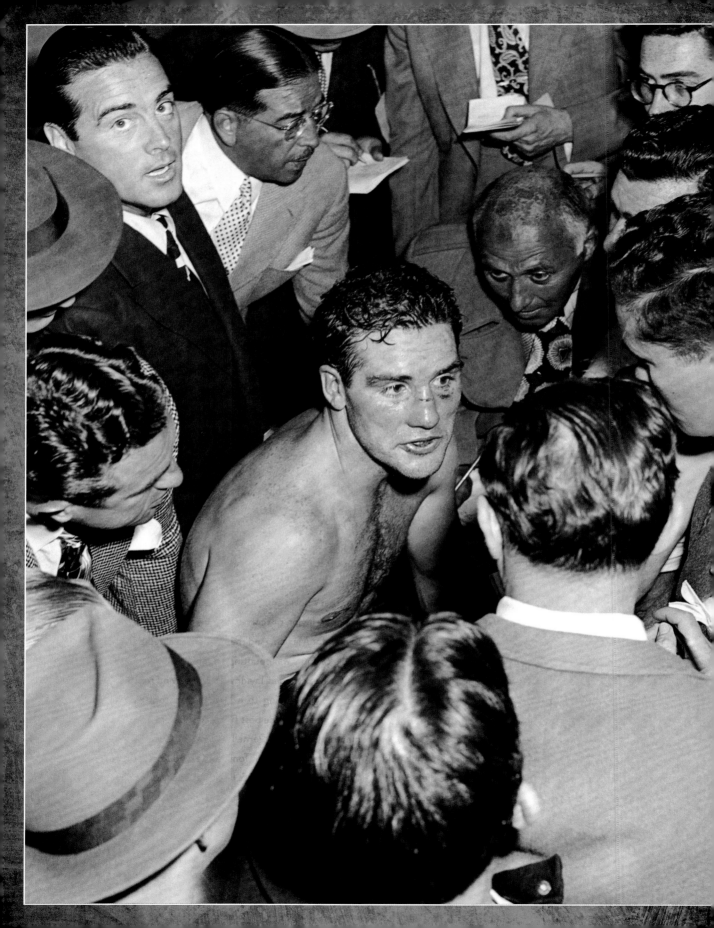

BILLY CONN

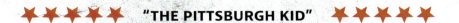 "THE PITTSBURGH KID" ★★★★★

PITTSBURGH, PA
BORN: October 8, 1917
DIED: May 29, 1993
HEIGHT: 6'1½"
RECORD: 63–11–1 (15 KOs)
TITLES WON: World Light Heavyweight Champion
HALL OF FAME INDUCTION: 1990

As great as Billy Conn was as a light heavyweight champion from 1939 to 1941, "The Pittsburgh Kid" will be forever known as the man who was three rounds away from dethroning the great Joe Louis in 1941.

For twelve rounds, Conn, who was outweighed by twenty-five and a half pounds, represented an impossible puzzle for Louis to solve. As he went back to his corner after the twelfth stanza, Conn was up on two scorecards and even on the third. His corner told him to fight smart and not get into a slugfest with "The Brown Bomber."

Conn didn't listen. He was so confident of victory that he felt he could close the show in style. He waded into battle in round 13 looking for the knockout. Late in the frame, there was indeed a knockout, but it was Louis scoring it. The fight was over: Louis had retained the title, and Conn could only wonder about what could have been. At least he could laugh about it.

"What's the sense of being Irish if you can't be dumb?" said Conn after the fight.

Fans and pundits wanted a rematch, but both Conn and Louis were called to serve in the US Army as World War II raged on. In 1946, they met again, but the time away from the ring had taken its toll on Conn, who was stopped in eight rounds. He fought only twice more, winning both bouts, before he retired in 1948.

Although his rivalry with Louis will always be the first thing that comes to mind for the proud Pittsburgh native, his career before those two fights deserves at least equal billing, considering his longtime status as the best 175-pounder on the planet.

Conn started with a disappointing 7–6 in his first thirteen fights, but once he got into a groove, the slick boxer put together a run that was nearly unstoppable. He beat the likes of Fred Apostoli, Solly Krieger, Melio Bettina, and Gus Lesnevich before he ran into Louis at the Polo Grounds in New York City.

TERENCE CRAWFORD

 "BUD"

OMAHA, NE
BORN: September 28, 1987
HEIGHT: 5'8"
RECORD: 41–0 (31 KOs)*
TITLES WON: World Champion at Lightweight,
Junior Welterweight, Welterweight, and Junior Middleweight

*As of press date

Before the highly anticipated welterweight SuperFight between the unbeatens Terence Crawford and Errol Spence in 2023, I was asked to give my thoughts on the matchup. In my opinion, it was an easy fight to break down.

Spence was a sniper who waited for opponents to slip up before making them pay from long range without getting his hands dirty. Crawford? He was Tony Montana at the end of *Scarface*, spraying bullets with abandon. When the dust cleared, either he got you or you got him.

After twelve rounds on July 29, 2023, Tony Montana—I mean, Terence Crawford—won. And what was supposed to be an evenly fought bout between the two best 147-pound boxers of this era wasn't even close. Crawford put Spence on the deck three times before the fight was stopped in the ninth round.

To date, it's been the defining moment of Crawford's career, but "Bud" has always been a level above when the bell rings.

A proud native of Omaha, Nebraska, he's considered that city's greatest sports franchise. Crawford fought his early career in relative obscurity, but as the wins piled up, fight fans slowly came on board and realized that he was something special. The "it" factor? Crawford simply loves to fight. He can outbox anybody, but he prefers to get into a scrap, and he has won every skirmish and battle.

The result has been world championships in four weight classes, two of them (at 140 and 147 pounds) undisputed—and he's far from done.

OSCAR DE LA HOYA

 "THE GOLDEN BOY"

LOS ANGELES, CA
BORN: February 4, 1973
HEIGHT: 5'10½"
RECORD: 39–6 (30 KOs)
TITLES WON: World Champion at Junior Lightweight, Lightweight, Junior Welterweight, Welterweight, Junior Middleweight, and Middleweight; 1992 Olympic Gold Medalist
HALL OF FAME INDUCTION: 2014

If your nickname is "The Golden Boy" and your looks ensure that you have as many female fans as male ones, there's a stereotype that goes along with that: You're a media creation who will never take on the tough challenges that go along with becoming a great in the sport of boxing.

Oscar De La Hoya heard it all. He even saw it happen to predecessor Sugar Ray Leonard. But when he came home from the 1992 Barcelona Olympics with a gold medal, the East Los Angeles native had a plan to silence all those critics who didn't know what he had in his chest.

"I understood what it took," De La Hoya said of his career.

"Every fighter's goal is to be great, but not every fighter's goal is to be respected. And I wanted both. I wanted the respect, and I understood that if you want to earn respect, you have to fight the tough challenges.

"You're gonna win some, you're gonna lose some, but you're going to earn respect. And to me, that means more than any title or any record that I might have. I'm pretty proud of taking on all challenges, no matter what."

Mission accomplished: That plan led him to the International Boxing Hall of Fame in 2014. But let's not forget that there are titles to talk about: eleven in six weight classes, to be exact. As for the fights, the wins and losses, and everything in between, De La Hoya was the engine that drove boxing in the 1990s, when he was facing the likes of Genaro Hernandez, Julio César Chávez, Pernell Whitaker, Héctor Camacho, Ike Quartey, and Félix Trinidad.

Some might say that he started to slip in the next decade, but he still posted huge wins over Fernando Vargas and Ricardo Mayorga. His megafights with Shane Mosley, Bernard Hopkins, Floyd Mayweather Jr., and Manny Pacquiao also proved that he was no marketing creation.

No, Oscar De La Hoya was a true fighter.

JACK DEMPSEY

 **"THE MANASSA MAULER"**

MANASSA, CO
BORN: June 24, 1895
DIED: May 31, 1983
HEIGHT: 6'1"
RECORD: 53–6–8 (43 KOs)
TITLES WON: World Heavyweight Champion
HALL OF FAME INDUCTION: 1990

In the Roaring '20s, sports captivated the American imagination. Of the four biggest stars—Babe Ruth, Red Grange, Bobby Jones, and Jack Dempsey—no one was bigger than "The Manassa Mauler," who ruled the heavyweight division from 1919 to 1927 and made headlines every step of the way.

This wasn't easy, with sports fans' attention pulled in so many different directions. But given Dempsey's power and action-packed brawling style, it was easy to see why he was the protagonist in the first $5 million gates in boxing history.

Not bad for a young man who was on his own at age sixteen, living on trains and trying to make ends meet by working in mining towns and offering to fight anyone who dared to face him. Manager Jack "Doc" Kearns ultimately took him under his wing, and before Dempsey knew it, he was a heavyweight contender.

Although Dempsey was undersized for the weight class, his punch made up for any physical shortcomings. Any doubts about his ability to win the title were erased on July 4, 1919, when he knocked down six-foot-six-and-a-half-inch champion Jess Willard seven times and won the heavyweight championship.

Dempsey had little trouble in his first four title defenses against Billy Miske, Bill Brennan, Georges Carpentier, and Tommy Gibbons. In his fifth, against Argentine strongman Luis Firpo, the champ was knocked out of the ring in the first round. Dempsey got back in the ring and back on his feet, and he proceeded to stop Firpo in the second round of a fight that saw a total of eleven knockdowns in three minutes and fifty-seven seconds.

It was another star-making turn for Dempsey, but when he returned to the ring three years later in 1926, Gene Tunney took the title via unanimous decision. They met a second time a year later with the same result, but not before the infamous "Long Count" almost gave Dempsey the win.

Dempsey never fought again, but he remained active as an ambassador of the sport and was part of the inaugural class of the International Boxing Hall of Fame in 1990.

ROBERTO DURÁN

 **"MANOS DE PIEDRA"**

EL CHORRILLO, PANAMA
BORN: June 16, 1951
HEIGHT: 5'7"
RECORD: 103–16 (70 KOs)
TITLES WON: World Champion at Lightweight, Welterweight, Junior Middleweight, and Middleweight
HALL OF FAME INDUCTION: 2007

Roberto Durán laughed at me once. And no, I didn't do a thing about it. Then again, maybe he wasn't laughing *at* me; maybe he was laughing *with* me. After all, my colleague Thomas Hauser had just told him and his son, Robert Jr., about my lone fight in the New York Golden Gloves.

Long story short, that fight ended in sixty-three seconds, and I was the one unconscious on the canvas. Upon hearing that, the Panamanian legend bellowed loudly as he opened his arms wide. Every other fighter I've told the Golden Gloves story to has said, "Hey, you got in there, not many people would do that." Not Durán. His laugh said, "Dude, don't try this. You're not cut out for it." He's got that mean in him.

A street kid with "Hands of Stone," Durán was as pure a fighter as there's ever been. For all his ferocity and primal intensity, however, his technique was immaculate and sublime. Punches that landed had no effect, as he moved his head the slightest bit upon impact. When he returned fire, he showed that his nickname was well deserved.

"Nobody hit harder than Roberto Durán," said former world champion Vinny Pazienza. "Please believe me. No one hit harder than him."

A champion in four weight classes (lightweight, welterweight, junior middleweight, and middleweight), Durán compiled a 103–16 (seventy knockouts) record over the course of a career that spanned 1970 to 2001. He beat a host of superstars when he moved to the welterweight division and beyond, including Sugar Ray Leonard, Carlos Palomino, Pipino Cuevas, and Iran Barkley. However, most agreed that he was at his best when he ruled the lightweight division.

At 135 pounds, Durán was unstoppable. He avenged his first pro loss to Esteban De Jesús twice and successfully defended the title he took from Ken

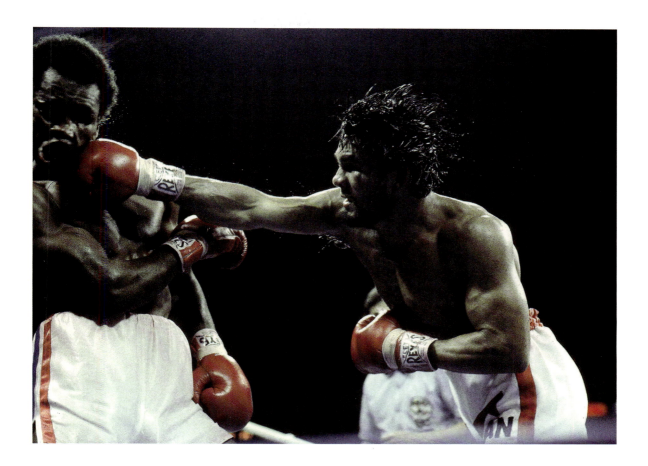

Buchanan in 1972 twelve times, with eleven of those wins by knockout.

Durán's move up in weight gave opponents some physical advantages, but the equalizer for the Panamanian was greater acclaim and paydays as he faced off with a trio of greats (Leonard, Thomas Hearns, Marvin Hagler) that, along with Durán, collectively became known as the Four Kings. He beat Leonard in their first fight but lost the next two—most famously, the "No Más" bout in late 1980, where Durán quit in the eighth round.

The controversy over that bout followed the king of machismo until he redeemed himself with a knockout of Davey Moore for the junior middleweight crown in 1983. His next two fights were with Hagler and Hearns. Durán lost to the future hall-of-famers, but he won eight of his next nine, culminating with what many consider his last great performance: an upset defeat of Iran Barkley for the middleweight title that proved he still had it at the age of thirty-seven, twenty-five pounds north of his prime fighting weight.

That's the stuff legends are made of.

BOB FITZSIMMONS

★★★★★ "RUBY ROBERT" ★★★★★

HELSTON, CORNWALL, ENGLAND
BORN: May 26, 1863
DIED: October 22, 1917
HEIGHT: 5′11½″
RECORD: 61–8–4, 6 NC (57 KOs)
TITLES WON: World Heavyweight Champion, World Light Heavyweight Champion, World Middleweight Champion
HALL OF FAME INDUCTION: 1990

Bob Fitzsimmons may not have invented the solar plexus punch, but he certainly perfected it. He used the blow just under the heart to win the heavyweight title from James J. Corbett in March 1897.

It was just one of many notable occurrences in the colorful career of "Ruby Robert," whose bout with Corbett was the first fight filmed and released to the public. The Brit was also boxing's first three-division champion.

The strange thing is, he never looked the part of a heavyweight champion. He was already in his mid-thirties when he won the title, his hair was thinning, and his skinny lower body deceptively hid the amazing strength that he'd built during his time as a blacksmith—the same strength that had produced an impressive 93 percent KO rate.

History will always remember Fitzsimmons for his exploits among the big boys of the heavyweight division, but many observers believed he was at his best as a middleweight, when he battled "Nonpareil" Jack Dempsey in 1891 en route to his first crown. Six years later, he shocked the world by upsetting Corbett, and although Fitzsimmons lost his title in 1899, he still had enough in the tank in 1903 to drop down to light heavyweight and win his third divisional title by decisioning George Gardiner.

And no matter where fans think he did his best work, it was a heck of a career for this former blacksmith, who was a member of the International Boxing Hall of Fame's inaugural class of 1990.

GEORGE FOREMAN

 "BIG GEORGE"

MARSHALL, TX
BORN: January 10, 1949
DIED: March 21, 2025
HEIGHT: 6'4"
RECORD: 76–5 (68 KOs)
TITLES WON: Two-time World Heavyweight Champion; 1968 Olympic Gold Medalist
HALL OF FAME INDUCTION: 2003

F. Scott Fitzgerald famously wrote, "There are no acts in American lives." The life of George Foreman disputes that notion: He's been an Olympic gold medalist; a surly, intimidating, and lovable heavyweight titleholder; an underdog comeback champ who won the belt twenty years after his first reign; a father; a preacher; and the namesake of a beloved grill that earned him tens of millions in retirement.

That's living.

"Nobody's got a monopoly on life and death," said Foreman. "And it's not how long you live, it's the quality of the life you live, and I'm thankful for the quality of life."

The Texas native was built like a brick wall, and he hit opponents like he had those bricks in his gloves. Foreman first shocked the world in 1973 when he knocked down Joe Frazier six times en route to a second-round stoppage and the world heavyweight crown. When he then handed top contender Ken Norton a similarly brutal defeat, fans feared for Muhammad Ali's safety as the pair traveled to Zaire for 1974's "Rumble in the Jungle."

"That's the sad thing about it," he said. "I had cleaned Ken Norton out, wiped out George Chuvalo, who had gone twelve rounds with [Ali], and I knocked them out.

"Muhammad Ali was no concern. I figured I'd knock him out in maybe two, three rounds, at the most. And what made me so good against Joe Frazier was that I was afraid of him. And what made me so terrible was that I had literally no respect for Muhammad Ali. None."

Ali stunned Foreman, knocking him out in the eighth round. Foreman's aura of invincibility was shattered. After a 1977 loss to Jimmy Young, he left the sport and became a preacher. But ten years later, Foreman decided to raise some money for his church by staging a comeback. This version of "Big George" was a stark contrast to the first, and fans embraced the affable, mellowed Texan.

He could still fight, though: On November 5, 1994, at the age of forty-five, he knocked out Michael Moorer to regain the world heavyweight title. As HBO play-by-play man Jim Lampley exclaimed that night, "It happened."

It certainly did.

BOB FOSTER

ALBUQUERQUE, NM
BORN: April 27, 1942
DIED: November 21, 2015
HEIGHT: 6'3"
RECORD: 56–8–1 (46 KOs)
TITLES WON: World Light Heavyweight Champion
HALL OF FAME INDUCTION: 1990

Mike Quarry wasn't doing too badly in his first shot at the light heavyweight title in 1972. The younger brother of heavyweight contender Jerry Quarry wasn't going to hurt champion Bob Foster, but with his speed and footwork, he was confident he could outbox him.

Unfortunately for the Californian, Foster always had an equalizer. As the two exchanged punches in the closing seconds of the fourth round, the champ detonated it—a left hook that put Quarry down and out.

Another win, another knockout, another title defense for Foster, who was not only one of boxing's great punchers, but also one of the best light heavyweights to ever step into the ring.

In May 1968, Albuquerque's Foster won the 175-pound title by knocking out Dick Tiger. The steel-chinned Nigerian had only ever been stopped once, due to a thumb injury. Foster was the only man in Tiger's eighty-two professional fights to knock him out.

That's a different kind of power, and it came not from a fighter chiseled out of stone with muscles upon muscle, but from a lanky six-foot-three battler who was able to drop bombs from any angle and with either fist.

Once champion, Foster was untouchable, successfully defending his crown fourteen times, from 1968 to 1974. His dominance impressed hardcore boxing fans, but the general public wanted to see heavyweights, so Foster twice moved up in weight to challenge for the title. He lost both bouts—to none other than Joe Frazier and Muhammad Ali—but his place among the greats of the sport was already more than secure.

JOE FRAZIER

★★★★★ "SMOKIN' JOE" ★★★★★

PHILADELPHIA, PA
BORN: January 12, 1944
DIED: November 7, 2011
HEIGHT: 5'11¼"
RECORD: 32–4–1 (27 KOs)
TITLES WON: World Heavyweight Champion; 1964 Olympic Gold Medalist
HALL OF FAME INDUCTION: 1990

Joe Frazier sang to me once. Yes, I know he sang to a lot of people when he was the frontman of Joe Frazier and The Knockouts, but this song was for me as we chatted before the airing of a 2005 documentary on his life.

"It was something in my life all along," said Frazier. "We came from a very religious family. If you didn't sing on Sunday, when you got back to the house, Mom would want to know why. And she kept a switch in corner. 'Why you can't sing? You think you're better than anybody else?' 'No, mom, I . . .' *Schhwupp.* 'You gonna sing next Sunday?' 'Yes ma'am.'"

Joe could sing, but I'm not being disrespectful when I say that he was a better fighter than singer. Who else could stop the world for an entire night like he and Muhammad Ali did when they met at Madison Square Garden on March 8, 1971?

"The part about stopping the world, I didn't pay one ounce of attention to that," said Frazier. "My job was to watch him and figure out what he was doing; otherwise, he was gonna wrap me up and throw me away. I didn't focus on all the great entertainers that were there or on the crowd—some of them were with me, some of them with him. My job was to concentrate on what [my trainer] Yank [Durham] told me in the corner and to get the job done."

That night in New York City, Frazier—a boxer who had already delivered some great performances en route to a spotless 26–0 record and the world heavyweight championship—handed the 31–0 Ali his first pro loss, punctuating matters with a fifteenth-round knockdown to ensure that the Fight of the Century lived up to the hype.

Still, Frazier remained the humble family man from Beaufort, South Carolina, who was now calling Philadelphia home. The less-than-ideal conditions in which he grew up had a positive side effect: They instilled in him a work ethic that earned him an Olympic gold medal in 1964 and the world heavyweight championship in 1968.

"Smokin' Joe" also possessed a pretty decent left

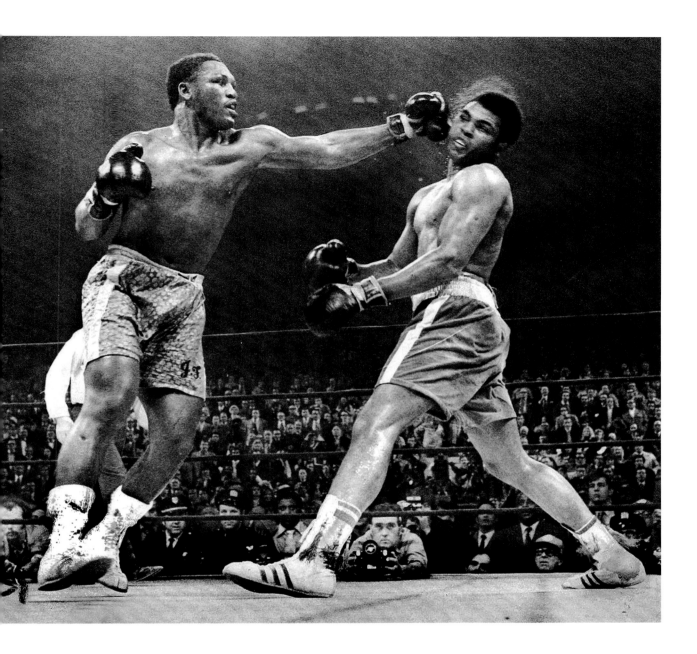

hook, which may have been the most potent weapon in boxing history. Frazier threw it with abandon, and when it hit its mark, it didn't just land—it erupted. Frazier's hook led him to victories over Jerry Quarry, Bob Foster, Jimmy Ellis, Oscar Bonavena, and George Chuvalo.

But he saved his best for Ali, the rival he shared three bouts with—including the epic "Thrilla in Manila" in 1975. Ali took two of the three, but Frazier's efforts allowed him to hold his head high.

In fact, it's safe to say that there's no Muhammad Ali without Joe Frazier because, to be great, a fighter needs a great dance partner.

Ultimately, though, "Smokin' Joe" wanted a different legacy for himself.

"I want them to remember that I was fair, [I was] concerned, and I had a lot of love in my heart for people," he said. "That's where it's at. I wanted to be fair to everybody, and I want everybody to have a chance."

TYSON FURY

★★★★★ "THE GYPSY KING" ★★★★★

MANCHESTER, ENGLAND
BORN: August 12, 1988
HEIGHT: 6'9"
RECORD: 34–2–1 (24 KOs)*
TITLES WON: World Heavyweight Champion

*As of press date

Tyson Fury was in the middle of nowhere—a hotel room in Gatineau, Quebec, Canada. Just 24 years old, the Brit was already a star at home, but he wanted to conquer the rest of the world, starting with the United States.

That led him to the Great White North, where he was staying before making the trip south to New York City to face former cruiserweight champion Steve Cunningham on April 20, 2013. It was a highly anticipated debut, but few knew how Fury, who was named after Mike Tyson, would impact the game. "The Gypsy King" knew, though.

"There's nobody who's come, grabbed the division, and kicked it on its head," Fury said. "And that's where I come in. I'm not all talk. You get these British hype jobs and these European fighters and they can't really fight. Let's be real. I'm a realist. If I couldn't fight, I'd say I can't fight. I like to be real, I don't want to con anybody and I can fight. I can fight southpaw, orthodox, in close, outwards, upside down—whatever you want to do, I can do. I throw combinations, I punch hard, and I'm an exciting fighter. So here we are, the savior of the heavyweight division."

Go ahead and add oracle to Fury's job description, because he dominated his weight class for the next eleven years and became an in-demand personality around the globe, complete with memoirs, a reality show, and all the controversies that come with being a mainstay in the public eye.

But to reach superstar status, he had to perform in the ring, and that he did. He rose off the canvas to stop Cunningham in their fight, just like he had to in his instant classic with Deontay Wilder in their first bout in 2018, which saw the two warriors produce an electrifying draw. But if you get Fury down, you can't keep him there: they fought twice more, with Fury knocking out the American both times.

Wins over Wladimir Klitschko (who he defeated for the heavyweight title in 2015), Dillian Whyte, and Derek Chisora added to his claim as the best of his era, and while a pair of defeats to Oleksandr Usyk in 2024 put the first losses on his 34-0-1 record, Fury's legacy as an all-time great is secure.

JOE GANS

 "THE OLD MASTER"

BALTIMORE, MD
BORN: November 25, 1874
DIED: August 10, 1910
HEIGHT: 5'6½"
RECORD: 147–10–16, 6 NC (101 KOs)
TITLES WON: World Lightweight Champion
HALL OF FAME INDUCTION: 1990

They called Joe Gans "The Old Master," and there was no more fitting nickname for a boxer who had studied the art he practiced from 1891 to 1909.

Perhaps the best athlete in the world during that time, Gans was also Black, which meant he had to fight not only his opponents, but also the racism running rampant throughout the United States. Despite this added obstacle, Gans was as cool under pressure as anyone could be, frequently using his skill and his smarts to beat his opponents.

Nat Fleischer, founder of *The Ring* magazine, named Gans the greatest lightweight ever in 1958. At that time—and even earlier—few would argue. Gans won 147 bouts, 101 by knockout, and lost only 10 times; his record included names such as Jimmy Britt, Jack Blackburn, Mike Sullivan, "Barbados" Joe Walcott, Sam Langford, Terry McGovern, and Frank Erne.

For all his technical brilliance, Gans was also as gritty as they came when the occasion called for it. This was never more evident than when he faced Battling Nelson in 1906. The two traded blows in the heat of Goldfield, Nevada, for forty-two rounds. Gans, the lightweight champion, won by disqualification but received only $11,000 for his trouble. Nelson, a white man, received twice as much for his purse.

The two met twice more in 1908, and Gans lost both. By then, the Baltimore native had contracted tuberculosis and was getting weaker by the day. On August 10, 1910, the disease took Gans's life at just thirty-five years old.

ARTURO GATTI

 "THUNDER"

MONTREAL, QUEBEC, CANADA
BORN: April 15, 1972
DIED: July 11, 2009
HEIGHT: 5′8″
RECORD: 40–9 (31 KOs)
TITLES WON: World Champion at Junior Lightweight and Junior Welterweight
HALL OF FAME INDUCTION: 2013

All boxers give something of themselves to the sport. Arturo Gatti gave everything—every time he stepped through the ropes.

That attitude thrilled fans from 1991 to 2007, as Gatti won world titles in two weight classes while competing in wars that kept his diehard followers on the edge of their seats from start to finish. He was boxing's human highlight film, but watching those fights always begged the question: What was the morning after like?

"Well, I don't see the daylight because my eyes are swelled up," Gatti laughed, also pointing out that, when his alarm rang, he started throwing punches because he thought a round had started.

The Montreal native joked about it, but that didn't make watching him in the ring any easier for his friends and family.

"People go, 'Oh, he was in such a great fight,' and I say, 'Yeah, for you guys it's a great fight. But not for me. This is my blood. His blood is my blood,'" recalled his brother, Joe Gatti. "I was there at a lot of his fights with tears."

The crazy thing is, Gatti didn't have to bite down on his mouthpiece, tuck his chin, and wade into a slugfest. As he proved in his wins over Tracy Harris Patterson and Terron Millett, Gatti could box brilliantly when he wanted to—but more often than not, he didn't want to. If he got hit, he wanted to hit his opponent back twice as hard. The resulting battles were instant classics with Wilson Rodriguez, Gabriel Ruelas, and Ivan Robinson.

But no fights captured who Gatti was better than his trilogy with Micky Ward. No titles were on the line, but each man fought as if far, far more was at stake. Ward took their first fight in 2002, but Gatti bounced back and won the next two, forever linking the two friendly rivals.

Tragically, Gatti died in Brazil on July 11, 2009, at the age of thirty-seven. The beloved "Thunder" was posthumously inducted into the International Boxing Hall of Fame in 2013, his first year of eligibility.

WILFREDO GÓMEZ

 "BAZOOKA"

LAS MONJAS, PUERTO RICO
BORN: October 29, 1956
HEIGHT: 5'5½"
RECORD: 44–3–1 (42 KOs)
TITLES WON: World Champion at Junior Featherweight, Featherweight, and Junior Lightweight
HALL OF FAME INDUCTION: 1995

Wilfredo Gómez was a joy to watch in the ring. Spectating his fights was almost like playing a video game or watching an action movie in which every punch was designed not just to land, but to end the fight.

The Puerto Rican star was far from a mindless brawler, though. His combination punching was dynamic and flawless, and the pressure he put on could crack the resolve of the sturdiest opposition. And yes, if he caught an opponent clean, a ten-count usually followed. All these attributes combined made him an icon on his island, a three-division world champion, and a member of the International Boxing Hall of Fame.

It all started in Las Monjas, where Gómez fell in love with boxing and became an amateur star. He won ninety-six of ninety-nine bouts while also competing in the 1972 Olympics. Gómez was eliminated from the Munich games early on, and although it was tempting to stick around for the 1976 games, he turned pro to aid his family financially. That turned out to be the wisest choice of all.

Now free to implement his pro style without the restraints of the amateur system, Gómez became a terror at 122 pounds. His nickname, "Bazooka," was more than appropriate. Following a draw in his pro debut on November 16, 1974, he won his next thirty-two fights—all by knockout.

During this stretch, Gómez won the WBC junior featherweight title and defended it thirteen times, including once against another future hall-of-famer, Carlos Zárate. It got to the point that he had practically cleaned out the division, leading him to move up to the featherweight division to challenge yet another man destined for the hall of fame: WBC champion Salvador Sánchez.

This fight didn't go so well for Gómez. He was halted by Sánchez in eight rounds, but he bounced back from his first defeat and returned to junior featherweight. He retained his 122-pound title four more times, most notably in a fourteen-round war with Lupe Pintor. "Bazooka" wanted that featherweight belt, though. On March 31, 1984, he got it by beating Juan La Porte over twelve rounds in his first fight to ever go the distance.

Later that year, Gómez lost the belt to Azumah Nelson (another future hall-of-famer). He fought only four more times before hanging up the gloves for good in 1989.

HARRY GREB

★★★★★ "THE PITTSBURGH WINDMILL" ★★★★★

PITTSBURGH, PA
BORN: June 6, 1894
DIED: October 22, 1926
HEIGHT: 5'8"
RECORD: 261–16–19, 1 NC (49 KOs)
TITLES WON: World Middleweight Champion and American Light Heavyweight Champion
HALL OF FAME INDUCTION: 1990

Harry Greb went 45–0 in 1919. That's not a typo. And it's not a career record, either. In the span of just twelve months, the man known as "The Pittsburgh Windmill" fought forty-five times and won every single time.

That stat alone could have landed Greb a place in this book, even when accounting for the fact that he fought during an era with a much higher volume of fights. Stepping into the ring an average of 3.75 times a month for an entire year boggles the mind in *any* era. Triumphing in all of them defies reason altogether.

But Greb was a fighter at his core. When you consider that he stepped between the ropes 299 times over the course of his thirteen-year career, it's readily apparent that he loved what he did for a living. And he did most of it while blind in one eye.

So how did Greb get around a disability that would have crippled most boxers' chances of glory? By throwing punches in bunches round after round—hence, "The Pittsburgh Windmill" moniker. And if the punches didn't get you, Greb's adoption of less-than-legal tactics made him a nightmare opponent to face.

Fighting as often as he did, Greb faced and defeated the best of the best en route to his middleweight and light heavyweight titles, including Gene Tunney, Jack Dillon, Battling Levinsky, Tommy Gibbons, Maxie Rosenbloom, Mickey Walker, Tommy Loughran, Jimmy Slattery, and Tiger Flowers. In all, Greb squared off with sixteen fighters who joined him in the International Boxing Hall of Fame.

After a split-decision loss to Flowers in August 1926, Greb announced his retirement. Just two months later, complications from a seemingly routine

surgery on his nose caused Greb to die of heart failure at the age of thirty-two. But what a life he lived in those years. His body of work can be relived and celebrated through books and the newspaper reports of his fights, but no fight footage has been found; only some training clips showcase one of the sport's pound-for-pound best.

EMILE GRIFFITH

SAINT THOMAS, US VIRGIN ISLANDS
BORN: February 3, 1938
DIED: July 23, 2013
HEIGHT: 5'7½"
RECORD: 85–24–2, 1 NC (23 KOs)
TITLES WON: World Champion at Junior Middleweight, Welterweight, and Middleweight
HALL OF FAME INDUCTION: 1990

The stars were out at the Downtown Athletic Club in New York City. Former heavyweight contender Gerry Cooney was throwing an event for his F.I.S.T. foundation, and I had just gotten blown off for an interview. It was the late 1990s, and I was new to the game, so being asked how much I was going to pay to talk to LaMotta was a little discouraging.

Then I saw Emile Griffith and his ever-present smile, and all was well with the world again. All class, the former three-division champion couldn't have been nicer to this fan trying his darndest to be a boxing writer. When our conversation ended, I committed the cardinal sin that any budding journalist knows to avoid like the plague: I asked for an autograph. I stammered that I knew that it was highly unprofessional, but . . .

Griffith laughed, waved off my excuses, and signed my notepad.

That's how I'll always remember the Virgin Islands native, and I'm sure I'm not the only one who was the recipient of his kindness. That's just who he was—and if that's the legacy you leave, it doesn't really matter what you did in your professional life.

For more reasons than one, though, Griffith's professional life was one to remember. A gentle soul, perhaps it's not too surprising that he fell into boxing completely by accident. When his boss at the hat factory where he worked saw him without his shirt on, he was impressed by Griffith's physique and referred him to Gil Clancy's boxing gym. Thus the die was cast.

Impressive as an amateur, Griffith raised the bar significantly when he turned pro in 1958. He was a world welterweight champion just three years later, knocking out Cuban national Benny "Kid" Paret for the belt. Paret rallied hard to regain the title six months later, but in their third fight, on March 24, 1962, tragedy struck.

Griffith was incensed after Paret groped his buttocks and hurled homophobic slurs at him during the weigh-in, and what was supposed to be a rubber match quickly became a grudge match. In the twelfth round, Griffith stunned Paret and then fired off a flurry of punches at his foe, who was stuck in the corner. When referee Ruby Goldstein finally stopped the bout, it was too late. Paret slumped to the canvas and was rushed to the hospital, but he never regained consciousness.

Despite the abuse Paret had thrown at him, Griffith was devastated. Nonetheless, he forged ahead, and his career continued. Some say he never regained the killer instinct he'd had before the Paret tragedy, but Griffith was still an elite fighter who went on to win titles at 154 and 160 pounds, defeating the likes of Dick Tiger, Luis Rodríguez, Rubin "Hurricane" Carter, Nino Benvenuti, and Bennie Briscoe.

Most boxing fans don't blame him for what happened that night, but, sadly, the third Paret fight is the first thing many people think of when recalling Emile Griffith. It shouldn't be. He was so much more than that one night in Madison Square Garden, as this poignant reflection on the bitter irony of his boxing legacy demonstrates: "I kill a man, and most people understand and forgive me. However, I love a man, and to so many people, this is an unforgivable sin; *this* makes me an evil person."

MARVELOUS MARVIN HAGLER

BROCKTON, MA
BORN: May 23, 1954
DIED: March 13, 2021
HEIGHT: 5'9"
RECORD: 62–3–2 (52 KOs)
TITLES WON: World Middleweight Champion
HALL OF FAME INDUCTION: 1993

Marvelous Marvin Hagler (yes, his legal name) once said that if someone cut his head open, they would find a big boxing glove. That's how much he loved the sport and dedicated his life to it, even if it didn't always treat him right in return.

Take, for example, the reality that Hagler was ducked by world champions left and right early in his career, forcing him to build a 46–2–1 record before he was finally given a shot at Vito Antuofermo's middleweight crown in 1979, six years after he turned pro.

To add insult to injury, the judges ruled the fight a draw that day in Las Vegas, even though the vast majority of observers believed Hagler deserved the nod and the belt. He then had to win three more fights before he got another title shot, this one on September 27, 1980, against the man who took Antuofermo's belt, Alan Minter.

This time, Hagler didn't let the judges get involved. After bloodying and stopping Minter in three rounds, he made himself a world champion. This also made him an American who'd beaten a Brit in London. Fans threw bottles and other debris into the ring when the fight was stopped, requiring Hagler and his team to be escorted by police back to the locker room.

Finally, though, Hagler had the recognition he wanted. He went on to dominate a tough middleweight division, beating Mustafa Hamsho, Tony Sibson, Wilford Scypion, Juan Roldán, and John Mugabi en route to twelve successful title defenses.

Included were victories over fellow "Four Kings" Roberto Durán and Thomas Hearns, with the latter fight cemented in the history books as one of the greatest showdowns of all time.

Hagler's third-round stoppage of Hearns in 1985 was expected to be repeated when he faced the last of the kings, Sugar Ray Leonard, in 1987, but Leonard, who was returning from a nearly three-year retirement, pulled off the upset. Disgusted by the decision, which many believed he deserved, Hagler retired, moved to Italy, and never returned to the ring. He instead became an action movie star and a fixture at each year's hall of fame induction weekend in Canastota, New York, where he was enshrined in 1993.

REGINA HALMICH

KARLSRUHE, GERMANY
BORN: November 22, 1976
HEIGHT: 5'3"
RECORD: 54–1–1 (16 KOs)
TITLES WON: World Champion at Junior Flyweight, Flyweight, and Junior Bantamweight
HALL OF FAME INDUCTION: 2022

When women were given their rightful place in the International Boxing Hall of Fame in 2020, Regina Halmich should have been in the first class. Instead, she had to wait for 2022 to get her call to Canastota. For those who followed the career of the German pioneer of women's boxing, it was a long overdue honor.

You can start with the numbers to explain this oversight. Halmich retired in 2007 with a career record of 54-1-1. That's impressive, to say the least. What's more notable is that forty-four of those wins came in world title fights, as she became champion at 108, 112, and 115 pounds.

"At flyweight—and at a weight class above and below me—I boxed everyone who was number one to five in the rankings," said Halmich. "That's how it should be. Back then, there was only one large women's boxing association, so there weren't that many alternatives."

In the era before Claressa Shields and Katie Taylor brought the sport to unprecedented heights after their Olympic performances, few were paying attention to women's boxing—at least in the mecca of the sport, the United States.

In Germany, however, Halmich was box-office gold. From the moment Rod Stewart's "Da Ya Think I'm Sexy" blared from the arena speakers to accompany Halmich to the ring, fans were on their feet and roaring.

"As a woman, you not only have to be good at boxing, but you also have to be marketable," said Halmich.

"I was a tough fighter in the ring but also very womanly outside of the ropes. That certainly helped. And charismatic types are in demand. I must have brought all of that with me, and the audience could identify with me."

Halmich could fight, too, with a mix of boxing and brawling that had her well equipped for whatever she ran into on fight night. But fighting in the United States only once, in 1995, when she suffered her lone pro loss to Yvonne Trevino via cuts, likely hurt her with the voting members of the International Boxing Hall of Fame, which largely consists of members of the Boxing Writers Association of America. Luckily, the IBHOF finally got it right in 2022.

Better late than never.

NASEEM HAMED

 "PRINCE"

SHEFFIELD, ENGLAND
BORN: February 12, 1974
HEIGHT: 5'3"
RECORD: 36–1 (31 KOs)
TITLES WON: World Featherweight Champion
HALL OF FAME INDUCTION: 2015

Many critics would say Naseem Hamed wasn't one of the best featherweights of all time. Some would say he wasn't the best featherweight in the world during a career that spanned only a decade, from 1992 to 2002. I disagree.

Could he have fought on and reigned at the top longer than he did? Yes. Were there opponents he could have faced, such as Erik Morales and Junior Jones? Sure.

But in terms of impact and peak level, very few 126-pounders in boxing history can match Sheffield's "Prince."

The buzz started early—a quirky kid with a big mouth and even bigger power. I was working maintenance in the mid-1990s, and one of my coworkers was of Yemeni descent, like Hamed. He knew I was a boxing fan, so he handed me a paper bag with a VHS tape in it. It was a collection of Hamed's amateur and early pro fights. I was hooked.

Hamed did everything wrong when it came to technique: His balance was horrible, but when he landed a punch, it short-circuited opponents. He had brash charisma, to boot, and England embraced him immediately. Hamed won the WBO featherweight title in 1995, when he stopped countryman Steve Robinson in eight rounds. When Hamed made his US debut at Madison Square Garden in defense of the featherweight title he had already defended eight times, he absolutely took over New York City. Once the bell rang, he combined with Kevin Kelley for a wild bout that saw each man suffer three knockdowns before Hamed closed the show in the fourth round.

The takeover was complete.

Continuing to fight at home and abroad, and making headlines each step of the way, Hamed successfully defended his title six more times before he ran into Marco Antonio Barrera, who handed him his first and only loss via decision in 2001.

Hamed fought only once more, to defeat Manuel Calvo, before he retired and then received a place in the International Boxing Hall of Fame in 2015.

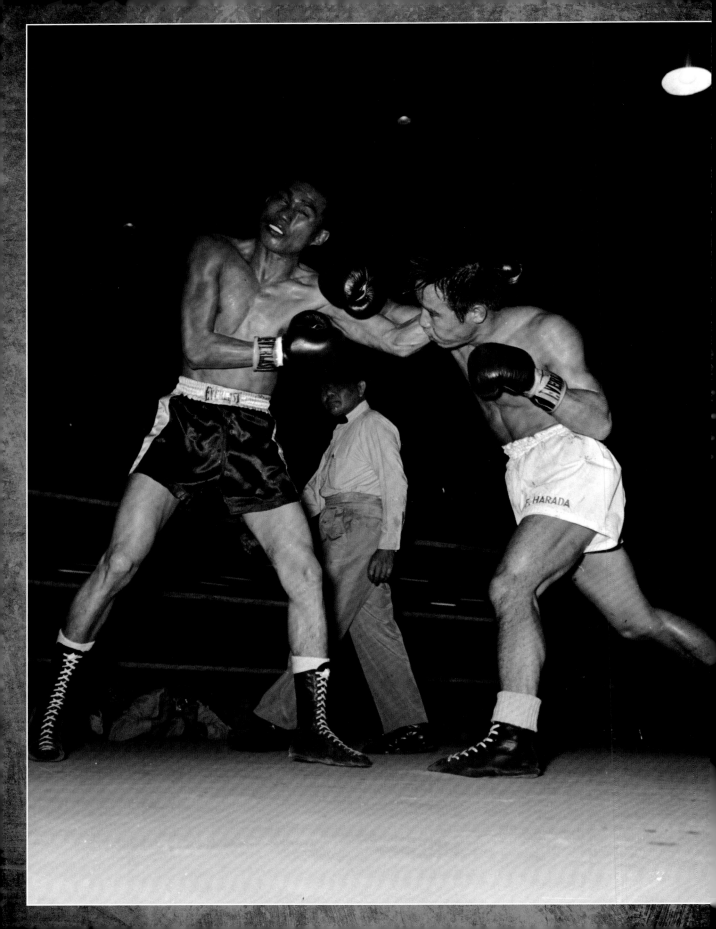

FIGHTING HARADA

TOKYO, JAPAN
BORN: April 5, 1943
HEIGHT: 5'3"
RECORD: 55–7 (22 KOs)
TITLES WON: World Champion at Bantamweight and Flyweight
HALL OF FAME INDUCTION: 1995

To this day, Japan has one of the richest boxing cultures in the world. But who was the best to ever do it from "The Land of the Rising Sun"?

Many believe it was Tokyo's Masahiko "Fighting" Harada.

An undisputed bantamweight and flyweight champion in his heyday in the 1960s, Harada captured the imagination of a nation as he chopped down opponent after opponent. In the process, Harada put a clear spotlight on the lighterweight classes that were often ignored internationally in favor of middleweights and heavyweights.

Harada didn't pack a heavyweight punch, notching only twenty-two knockouts in fifty-five wins. However, he was fast, his jab was sharp, and he made his opponents work. If you signed a contract to meet him in the ring, you were in for a fight.

In October 1962, he improved his record to 27–1 with an eleventh-round knockout of Pone Kingpetch that earned him the WBA flyweight title. Harada returned the belt to Kingpetch three months later, but bigger challenges awaited him in the bantamweight division. He chased after them with his characteristic intensity, ultimately earning a title fight with Brazilian great Éder Jofre in May 1965.

Entering the bout, Jofre sported a 47–0–3 record. After the fight, it was 47–1–3. Harada handed him his first loss and took his WBC bantamweight title. A year later, almost to the day, Harada repeated his win over the man he would one day join in the International Boxing Hall of Fame.

Harada reigned over the 118-pound weight class until February 1968, when he lost to Lionel Rose. Before he walked off into the sunset of retirement, he unsuccessfully challenged for Johnny Famechon's WBC featherweight title twice, still daring to be great to the end.

THOMAS HEARNS

 "THE HITMAN"

DETROIT, MI
BORN: October 18, 1958
HEIGHT: 6'1"
RECORD: 61–5–1 (48 KOs)
TITLES WON: World Champion at Welterweight, Junior Middleweight, Middleweight, Super Middleweight, and Light Heavyweight
HALL OF FAME INDUCTION: 2012

When you're a kid, you want to be good. But it's better to be cool. When you're playing sports, you want to have swagger like Joe Namath or to spit like Reggie Jackson. And if you were a boxing fan in my neighborhood in Brooklyn, you wanted to be like Thomas Hearns.

The lanky but lethal boxer known as "The Hitman" wasn't a trash talker or a flashy individual. On fight night, though, with his left hand hanging low by his side and his money-making right hand cocked and loaded, that was cool.

"It wasn't so much that I was cool; it was just that I was trying to create a memory for the people to have so that they would always remember that when Thomas Hearns came out there, be on alert—because the first few rounds, he's gonna give you a show and try to get the job done," Hearns said. "I wasn't trying to go the distance all the time. I wanted to go out there and get the job done. And if you didn't want to be in there, guess what? You go home early."

Hearns's right hand, homed in Detroit's Kronk Gym by his renowned trainer, Emanuel Steward, was the stuff of legend in the Motor City. The rest of the world got in on the secret in 1980, when he blasted out rugged Pipino Cuevas in two rounds to win the WBA welterweight title. It was the first of Hearns's five divisional crowns, and the spotlight came on and stayed on, making him a must-see for any self-respecting boxing fan.

Yes, the stats—including forty-eight knockouts in sixty-one wins and all those titles—are nice, but when the name Thomas Hearns comes up in conversation, it's the moments that live on forever.

His demolition of Roberto Durán. His classic bouts

with Sugar Ray Leonard. And, perhaps most notably, "The War" with Marvin Hagler in 1985, a fight that contained what most fans and pundits believe to be the best round in boxing history.

That first round was full of what Hearns was all about—power, skill, and heart. It's what he wanted to give the fans every night.

"If you put me in there, you put me in for a reason," said Hearns. "And whoever's in there and trying to stop me, he's got another thing coming because I don't quit that easy. I don't give up, and I won't go away. I'll put a show on. That was my thing."

LARRY HOLMES

 "THE EASTON ASSASSIN"

EASTON, PA
BORN: November 3, 1949
HEIGHT: 6'3"
RECORD: 69–6 (44 KOs)
TITLES WON: World Heavyweight Champion
HALL OF FAME INDUCTION: 2008

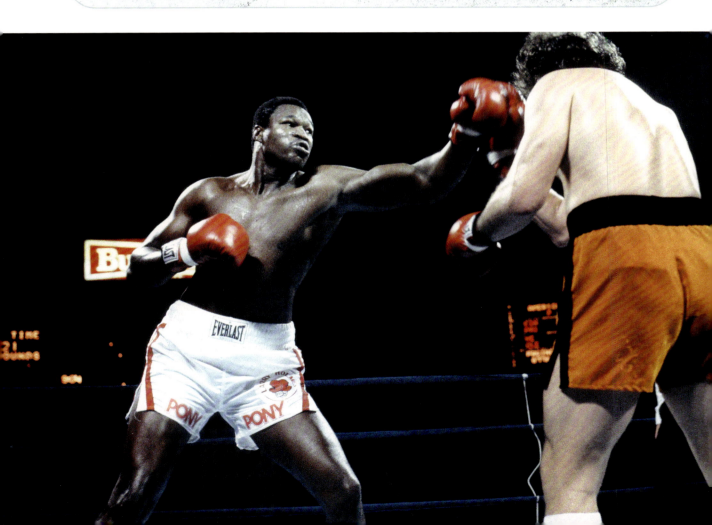

As Muhammad Ali's successor as heavyweight champion of the world, Larry Holmes knew he was never going to get the same recognition from the general public that "The Greatest" did.

By the time Holmes finished his seven-year reign at the top of the division, however, he'd earned his own place in the history of the greats, even if claiming that well-deserved praise was an uphill battle for "The Easton Assassin."

"I never thought I was the greatest fighter of all time, and I never said to myself I could be one of the greatest fighters of all time," Holmes said. "I don't get into that. I'm the luckiest one and the blessed one for all the times I spent in the ring and meeting the people that I've met. I'm just blessed. I did what I needed to do, and I didn't need to prove it to others. I needed to prove it to myself."

In his formative boxing years, Holmes was a sparring partner for Ali and Joe Frazier. Armed with those lessons learned in the gym, he began to make his way up the heavyweight ladder. He took on a host of tough foes—and beat them all—en route to a title fight against Ken Norton on June 9, 1978. What resulted was a fifteen-round, back-and-forth war, with the pair combining for perhaps the greatest round in heavyweight boxing history in the final frame. Holmes took a split decision and the belt, and the reign began.

Holmes completed a remarkable twenty title defenses, beating all comers, including his mentor, Ali, in 1980. It was a bittersweet victory for Holmes, who repeatedly asked the referee to stop the one-sided contest before Ali's corner threw in the towel after round 10.

Moving on, Holmes built his undefeated record to 48–0. He attempted to tie Rocky Marciano's 49–0 slate, but he was upset by Michael Spinks on September 21, 1985, and lost his title. The decision was controversial, as was the rematch, where Holmes's record stumbled further to 48–2.

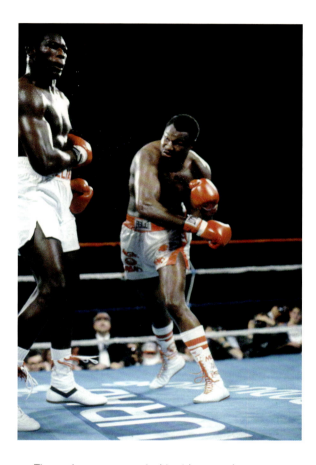

Three chances to regain his title over the next several years—against Mike Tyson, Evander Holyfield, and Oliver McCall—came up empty, but Holmes continued to fight. He ended his career on a four-fight winning streak at the age of fifty-two.

How did he manage it? Very likely due to what many consider to be the best jab in boxing history.

I once asked one-time prospect Derek Bryant, a Holmes sparring partner, what that jab was like. "I never saw it coming," said Bryant. "I only saw it going back."

EVANDER HOLYFIELD

"THE REAL DEAL"

ATLANTA, GA
BORN: October 19, 1962
HEIGHT: 6'2½"
RECORD: 44–10–2, 1 NC (29 KOs)
TITLES WON: World Champion at Heavyweight and Cruiserweight
HALL OF FAME INDUCTION: 2017

For all the talent Evander Holyfield had, which led him to an Olympic bronze medal and undisputed world championships at cruiserweight and heavyweight, the Georgia native's greatest attribute might have been his stubbornness.

He didn't agree.

"Stubborn?" he told me in 2006. "I don't think I'm stubborn."

At the time, "The Real Deal" was making another comeback, this time against journeyman Jeremy Bates. Holyfield had just finished citing chapter and verse about every time he'd been doubted and went on to silence such critics. That was the story of his career, the supposed "blown-up cruiserweight" who followed up winning that division's undisputed title by chasing after gold in the heavyweight division.

Few gave him a chance against the monsters among the big boys, who often dwarfed him. Again, Holyfield defied the odds, knocking out James "Buster" Douglas in the third round to win the heavyweight title in 1990. For the next dozen years, practically every fight was a big one, as Holyfield faced off with fellow elites George Foreman, Larry Holmes, Riddick Bowe, Mike Tyson, and Lennox Lewis. He lost the title and won it back twice, but that was the key takeaway: He always came back, determined that he could beat anyone of any size on any given night.

When Holyfield defied the odds and won, he never said, "I told you so."

"It's not so much for me to say that a person's wrong," Holyfield said. "It's just that your life identifies how you've been living. Right or wrong, your life shows what you've gone through. Whether you're a good or bad person, when you have trials and tribulations, it's how you handle them. I was born poor, but I didn't let that hold me down."

Instead, he was a shining example of what happens

when hard work meets opportunity. Holyfield made the most of all of them throughout his career, making him not just one of the best boxers of his era, but also one of the most popular.

Holyfield beat Jeremy Bates that night in 2006, went on to win five of his last eight bouts, and nearly won the heavyweight title again when he faced seven-foot-tall giant Nikolai Valuev, but he lost a highly controversial decision in 2008. Holyfield was forty-six years old and as lionhearted as ever—stubborn, too.

BERNARD HOPKINS

 "THE EXECUTIONER"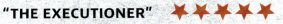

PHILADELPHIA, PA
BORN: January 15, 1965
HEIGHT: 6'1"
RECORD: 55–8–2, 2 NC (32 KOs)
TITLES WON: World Champion at Middleweight and Light Heavyweight
HALL OF FAME INDUCTION: 2020

There will never be another Bernard Hopkins. He was the man who could answer five interview questions with one response (I once clocked him at twelve minutes for one answer), the oldest fighter to win a world title (at forty-eight), and among the craftiest boxers to ever step into the ring.

It almost never happened: Hopkins spent fifty-six months in Graterford State Penitentiary for nine felonies. When he was released at age twenty-three in 1988, he had nine years of parole staring him in the face.

Hopkins turned to professional boxing but lost his debut to Clinton Mitchell. He didn't lose again for five years, though, when Roy Jones Jr. decisioned him in a middleweight title fight. "The Executioner" was undeterred. When he finally got his hands on the middleweight crown by beating Segundo Mercado in April 1995, he didn't let go of it for ten years.

With his legacy secure after making a record twenty middleweight title defenses, the Philadelphian was still hungry for more. In 2011, at the age of forty-eight, he defeated Jean Pascal for the light heavyweight championship. He went on to fight until 2016, when he was fifty-one years old.

Owner of wins over Jones Jr., Félix Trinidad, Oscar De La Hoya, Glen Johnson, William Joppy, Antonio Tarver, Winky Wright, and Kelly Pavlik, Hopkins was inducted into the International Boxing Hall of Fame in 2020.

It was a long road to Canastota, but what always impressed about Hopkins was his refusal to be complacent and his commitment to staying motivated.

"Motivation can come in all shapes and forms with me," he told me before the De La Hoya fight in 2004. "If I go outside and all my tires are slashed, that's motivation. When things run smoothly, somebody has to break a glass. Somebody has to do something. Some people need bumps in the road to make things happen. It [doesn't] always have to be downright dirty, ignorant stuff; it just has to be some type of motivation. In boxing, I'll never have a problem being motivated because there's always something in boxing, whether it's on my end, to be fair, or somebody else's end. There's always some motivation that will be brought to me, or some adversity will be brought to me."

And in true "B-Hop" style, Hopkins almost always came out a winner while doing things his way.

NAOYA INOUE

 "THE MONSTER"

KANAGAWA, JAPAN
BORN: April 10, 1993
HEIGHT: 5'5"
RECORD: 30–0 (27 KOs)*
TITLES WON: World Champion at Junior Featherweight, Bantamweight, Junior Flyweight, and Junior Bantamweight

*As of press date

It's become a ritual for boxing fans in North America. Set your clocks for 7:30 a.m. eastern time whenever "The Monster" is fighting.

That "Monster," Naoya Inoue, is already a legitimate star in his native Japan. There have been several of those over the years, but to translate that success around the world? That hasn't been seen since the days of the man considered to be Japan's best, Fighting Harada.

Some are already calling Inoue, who is not even thirty-five years old yet, the greatest boxer to emerge from the "Land of the Rising Sun." The reasons for such bold praise are simple: from a stylistic perspective, Inoue knocks people out. As I write this, he's finished twenty-seven of his thirty wins before the final bell. When this sharpshooter lands, people tend to fall on the ground in funny ways. And everybody loves knockouts.

But the thing with knockout artists is that most eventually run into someone who won't fall, who won't go away, and the bully gets bullied. So far, not Inoue. A dozen years into his career, he has fought plenty of opponents expected to test him—or even beat him—and he's passed those tests with flying colors.

One of only three fighters in the era of four championship belts in each division to be undisputed in two weight classes, and a four-division world champion overall, Inoue has already posted a hall-of-fame-worthy resume. And yet, despite defeating the likes of Nonito Donaire, Stephen Fulton, Jason Moloney, and Luis Nery, there is a distinct feeling that the best is still yet to come. I guess that means more early mornings for those of us in North America.

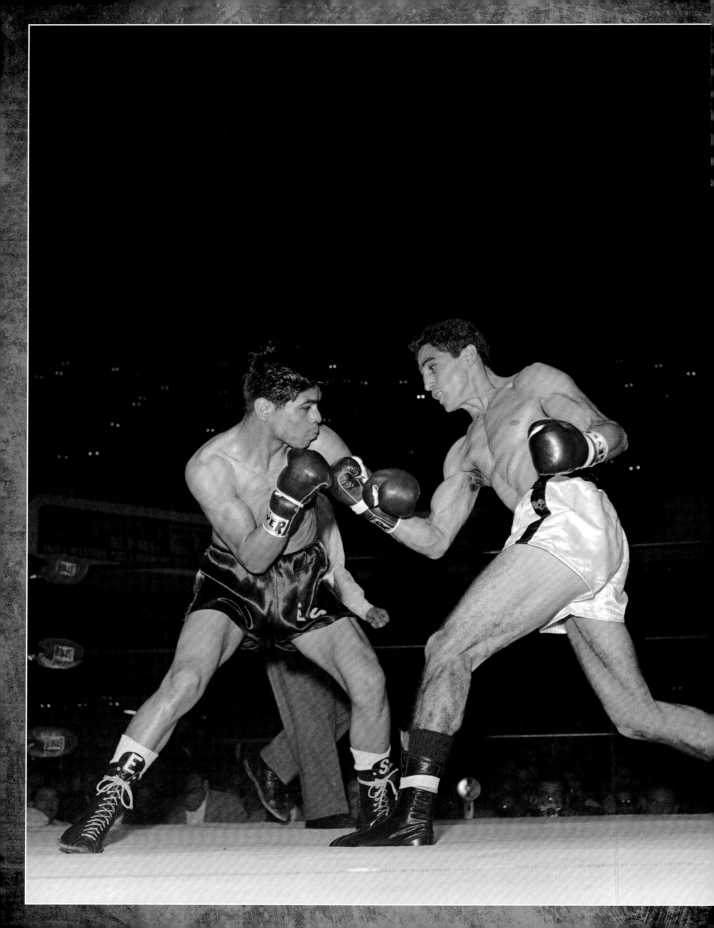

ÉDER JOFRE

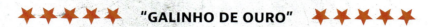

★★★★★ "GALINHO DE OURO" ★★★★★

SÃO PAULO, BRAZIL
BORN: March 26, 1936
DIED: October 2, 2022
HEIGHT: 5'4"
RECORD: 72–2–4 (50 KOs)
TITLES WON: World Champion at Bantamweight and Featherweight
HALL OF FAME INDUCTION: 1992

In mixed martial arts, Brazil has produced dozens of fighters who became stars abroad and icons at home. In boxing, the South American nation has not been as prolific. Sure, there was Acelino "Popó" Freitas, a former champion who had notable success in the United States. But when it comes to Brazilian all-time greats, there's only one name to consider: Éder Jofre.

A master boxer with legitimate power, Jofre first came to the attention of fight fans when he represented Brazil in the 1956 Olympics. Although he didn't strike gold in Melbourne, he got plenty of it in the pro ranks, which he entered in March 1957.

Fighting almost exclusively in his native São Paulo, Jofre built up an impressive 32–0–3 record before traveling to the United States in August 1960 for a bantamweight title elimination bout against José Medel. Despite the unfamiliar surroundings, Jofre was Jofre, knocking out Medel in the tenth round.

Two wins later, he was back in Los Angeles for a title fight, which he also won, knocking out Eloy Sanchez in six rounds for the bantamweight crown on November 18, 1960. Jofre defended his title eight times over the next four years before a pair of decision losses to fellow legend Fighting Harada in 1965 and 1966 cost him the crown.

Those were the only two losses of his career. After a three-year retirement, Jofre returned to rousing success, unlike most comebacks in boxing. He went 25–0 and won a featherweight title, which he defended once, before calling it quits for good after a twelve-round victory over Octavio Gomez on October 8, 1976.

In 1992, Jofre was inducted into the International Boxing Hall of Fame. He remains the only Brazilian boxer in the hall.

JACK JOHNSON

 "THE GALVESTON GIANT"

GALVESTON, TX
BORN: March 31, 1878
DIED: June 10, 1946
HEIGHT: 6'½"
RECORD: 53–11–8 (33 KOs)
TITLES WON: World Heavyweight Champion
HALL OF FAME INDUCTION: 1990

If this anecdote about Jack Johnson turns out to be just an urban legend, please don't tell me.

As the story goes, the first Black heavyweight champion was speeding—as was his habit—through the Jim Crow South and got pulled over. Told that the fine was $50, Johnson pulled out a hundred-dollar bill and handed it to the police officer.

"I can't cash that," said the officer.

"Keep the change," responded Johnson. "I'm coming back the same way I came through."

That was Jack Johnson. As the saying goes, he was one of one, a trailblazer who scoffed at the notion of not being any man's equal and never cowered to anyone—opponents, promoters, or the law.

That he was able to perform like he did while dealing with overwhelming racism was a feat in itself. But when it was just him and his opponent in the ring, defensive wizardry and sharp punches placed Johnson a level above crude foes who didn't have an answer for his fight IQ.

It wasn't easy, though. "The Galveston Giant" chased champion Tommy Burns around the globe—literally—before finally cornering the Canadian for a fight in Sydney, Australia. The day after Christmas, in 1908, Johnson defeated Burns (in a notably one-sided bout) to become the heavyweight champion of the world.

This didn't please the white establishment, but Johnson didn't care, even as the call went out for a "Great White Hope." Famed writer Jack London pleaded with former heavyweight champ James J. Jeffries to come out of retirement to defeat the new champ.

"Jim Jeffries must emerge from his alfalfa farm and remove the golden smile from Jack Johnson's face," wrote London. "Jeff, it's up to you!"

Jeffries made his return, but he was no match for Johnson, who stopped him in the first Fight of the Century on July 4, 1910. Sadly, the result provoked white violence around the country, leading to at least twenty deaths. It shows the world Johnson fought in, and it's not out of turn to surmise that this world eventually took him down.

In 1913, Johnson was arrested for violating the Mann Act, which was enacted to make it "a felony to engage in interstate or foreign commerce transport of 'any woman or girl for the purpose of prostitution or debauchery, or for any other immoral purpose.'"

The victim? Lucille Cameron, Johnson's girlfriend and future wife.

Johnson went into exile, fighting in France, Argentina, and, ultimately, Havana, Cuba, where he lost his title via twentieth-round knockout to Jess Willard.

In 1920, Johnson returned to the United States and surrendered to authorities to serve a sentence of less than a year. Upon his release, he fought sporadically until 1931 but never again reached the heights of his heyday.

In 2018, US President Donald Trump posthumously pardoned Johnson, who died in 1948 from injuries suffered in a car crash. For better or worse, he went back the way he went through—Jim Crows, Great White Hopes, Mann Acts, and Jack Londons be damned.

ROY JONES JR.

 "SUPERMAN"

PENSACOLA, FL
BORN: January 16, 1969
HEIGHT: 5′11″
RECORD: 66–10 (47 KOs)
TITLES WON: World Champion at Middleweight, Super Middleweight, Light Heavyweight, and Heavyweight
HALL OF FAME INDUCTION: 2022

How good was a prime Roy Jones Jr.? Good enough to play point guard for the Jacksonville Barracudas of the USBL the day of his 1996 super middleweight title defense against Éric Lucas.

Good enough to move from light heavyweight to heavyweight and take the WBA championship from John Ruiz.

And good enough to record a rap album that included a song with lyrics describing the first fifteen years of his professional career:

Can't be touched
Can't be stopped
Can't be moved
Can't be rocked
Can't be shook.

That was Roy Jones Jr. The Pensacola native bounced back from the disappointment of leaving the 1988 Seoul Olympics with only a silver medal (after one of the most outrageously controversial decisions in history against South Korea's Park Si-Hun), to become the most dominant force in the sport in the 1990s and early 2000s.

Whether it was speed, reflexes, fight IQ, or power, Jones had an answer for everything an opponent brought to the ring. His masterful, yet unorthodox, boxing skills set him apart and led him to world titles in four weight classes (middleweight, super middleweight, light heavyweight, and heavyweight) by beating the likes of Bernard Hopkins, James Toney, Vinny Pazienza, Mike McCallum, and Virgil Hill, but he could get mean when he needed to.

That was certainly the case in his rematch with Montell Griffin in August 1997. A little more than four months earlier, Jones had been controversially disqualified for hitting a downed Griffin, resulting in his first loss in thirty-five pro fights. In the rematch, Jones was taking matters into his own hands.

"We did see an RJ that we never had seen before,"

said Jones, who said the goal that night was simple. "The goal then was to kill him, if necessary."

Jones needed just two minutes and thirty-one seconds to end Griffin's night. If I were making the pick, I'd say it was the best performance of his career. He's not so sure.

"Toney, Ruiz, there are a lot of times," Jones said. "Even if you look at the Jeff Lacy fight, I had some pretty damn fast hands in that fight, so I don't know."

What we do know is that Jones's legacy as an all-time great was cemented on the night of March 1, 2003, when he defeated Ruiz for the heavyweight title. It wasn't the most spectacular fight in terms of action, but it was another brilliant performance for Jones. He wasn't able to reach those heights again: The move back down from heavyweight to light heavyweight came too soon, resulting in losses in three of his next four fights to Antonio Tarver (twice) and Glen Johnson.

Yet in a strange turn of events, the boxer once dubbed "Reluctant Roy" by critics showed just how much fighting spirit he had. He continued to compete until 2023, his love of the game superseding his love of money, fame, or glory.

STANLEY KETCHEL

 **"THE MICHIGAN ASSASSIN"**

GRAND RAPIDS, MI
BORN: September 14, 1886
DIED: October 15, 1910
HEIGHT: 5'9"
RECORD: 49–5–3, 2 NC (46 KOs)
TITLES WON: World Middleweight Champion
HALL OF FAME INDUCTION: 1990

John Lardner's lede was epic, a classic all writers should aspire to. Writing in the May 1954 issue of *True* magazine, he started his profile of Stanley Ketchel as follows:

Stanley Ketchel was twenty-four years old when he was fatally shot in the back by the common-law husband of the lady who was cooking his breakfast.

His murderers were both convicted in 1911, but that didn't bring back "The Michigan Assassin," who had already established himself as an all-time great at age twenty-four, before he'd even reached his fighting prime.

Despite Ketchel's youth, he knew well what it meant to fight, having run away from home at the age of twelve. By the time he was sixteen, he was fighting in unsanctioned boxing matches against all comers.

This unorthodox start served him well when he turned pro in 1903. He won thirty-six of his first forty-one fights. By 1908, he was a middleweight champion and one of the sport's most popular figures. Ketchel was aggressive in the ring, and if he landed with one of his punches, a fight could be over in a split second.

That power not only led him to wins over fellow middleweights like longtime rival Billy Papke, but it also allowed him to fight opponents who dwarfed him in size, such as heavyweight champion Jack Johnson.

Rumor had it that when the bout took place on October 16, 1909, Johnson was going to carry Ketchel, who was giving up thirty-five pounds, the twenty-round distance so the folks selling film of the fight got their money's worth. Ketchel had other ideas. He flipped the script and dropped Johnson in round 12. The incensed champion rose to his feet and knocked Ketchel out—removing two of his teeth in the process—but the fact remains that he shocked both Johnson and the boxing world that night.

His popularity untouched, Ketchel was back in the ring five months later. However, he would only fight five more fights before his tragic murder, leaving fans forever wondering what could have been.

WLADIMIR KLITSCHKO

 "DR. STEELHAMMER"

KYIV, UKRAINE
BORN: March 25, 1976
HEIGHT: 6'6"
RECORD: 64–5 (53 KOs)
TITLES WON: World Heavyweight Champion
HALL OF FAME INDUCTION: 2021

One of my favorite memories of Wladimir Klitschko dates to when he and his brother, Vitali, came to New York in 2004 to speak with the media about themselves and their careers. The Ukrainians were equally touted top-level boxers, both bona-fide stars in Europe. Outside the ring, however, there was a clear delineation between big brother and little brother.

Wladimir was fine with that.

"He has three kids," he said of Vitali, "two by his wife and one sitting next to him."

It was clear that Vitali, a heavyweight champion who went on to become the Mayor of Kyiv, was his idol. But Wladimir was always his own man, even as he was growing up and getting into the occasional scrap.

"I never used my brother to protect myself," said Wladimir. "I always tried to take care of those things myself. Sometimes it worked out bad because I came home with bruises under my eyes and a broken nose, but it's okay."

His boxing career turned out more than okay. An Olympic gold medal winner in 1996, "Dr. Steelhammer" was destined for greatness, despite some hiccups along the way—namely, upset losses to Ross Puritty, Corrie Sanders, and Lamon Brewster that had some questioning whether Klitschko was as good as he appeared.

He was. In fact, he was better. Klitschko dominated his era, making nineteen defenses of his WBO heavyweight title and eighteen defenses of his IBF title. This run of excellence was eclipsed only by Joe Louis and Larry Holmes. It wasn't a surprise, then, when Klitschko (who defeated Chris Byrd, Ray Mercer, Samuel Peter, Hasim Rahman, David Haye, and Alexander Povetkin, and then avenged his loss to Brewster) made it into the International Boxing Hall of Fame in his first year of eligibility, in 2021. Fittingly, he was right back at big bro Vitali's side, who had been inducted three years earlier.

JAKE LaMOTTA

★★★★★ "THE BRONX BULL" ★★★★★

BRONX, NY
BORN: July 10, 1922
DIED: September 19, 2017
HEIGHT: 5′8″
RECORD: 83–19–4 (30 KOs)
TITLES WON: World Middleweight Champion
HALL OF FAME INDUCTION: 1990

When a new generation thinks of Jake LaMotta, the first picture that pops into their head may very well be a motion picture—specifically, *Raging Bull*, an all-time classic film that saw Robert De Niro win a Best Actor Oscar for his portrayal of the former middleweight champion.

It wasn't a flattering portrait of the hall-of-famer, nor was it inaccurate. But despite his shortcomings outside the ring, LaMotta was an elite middleweight during his time inside it, with a legendary toughness perhaps not equaled before or since.

How tough was he? For starters, he fought Sugar Ray Robinson six times, even handing the pound-for-pound king his first pro loss in their second fight (although he lost the other five). In his post-career comedy act, LaMotta's go-to line was, "I fought Sugar Ray so often, I almost got diabetes."

The steel-chinned LaMotta also proved his toughness in his second middleweight title defense against Laurent Dauthuille in September 1950. Down on all scorecards heading into the fifteenth and final round, he needed a knockout to keep his title. He got it, swarming the Frenchman and finishing him with thirteen seconds left in the fight.

Unfortunately, toughness and a hard-to-decipher, pressure-based style weren't enough for him to get a shot at the title in the first place. LaMotta initially resisted playing ball with the mob that largely ran the sport in the 1950s, but he eventually gave in and threw his 1947 fight with Billy Fox in order to get his title opportunity. Two years later, he got it; he made the most of it, stopping Marcel Cerdan in nine rounds.

Clearly, LaMotta's story was a complicated one, but it was a long one, too. He lived to the age of ninety-five. Toughness.

SAM LANGFORD

CAMBRIDGE, MA
BORN: March 4, 1886
DIED: January 12, 1956
HEIGHT: 5′7½″
RECORD: 210–43–53, 8 NC (126 KOs)
TITLES WON: None
HALL OF FAME INDUCTION: 1990

One of boxing's most shameful facts is that Sam Langford never won a world championship. And it wasn't because the Nova Scotia native wasn't good enough—quite the contrary. During his twenty-four years in the ring and more than 300 recorded bouts, of which he won 210, Langford was actually too good for his own good.

And he was Black.

Although white challengers got shots at titles from lightweight to heavyweight, Langford was forced to simply face and beat whoever was willing to step into the ring with him. He got one shot at a title when he met "The Barbados Demon," Joe Walcott, for the welterweight championship in 1904, but a draw verdict was rendered in a fifteen-rounder that many believed Langford won.

That was the extent of world title fights for Langford, a brutal puncher and a skilled boxer who found willing dance partners in the other Black fighters being ignored by the champions of that time.

Langford fought Harry Wills eighteen times and also racked up double digits in battles with Sam McVey and Joe Jeannette. For the record, he did get into the ring with world champions such as Jack Johnson, Joe Gans, Stanley Ketchel, and Philadelphia Jack O'Brien, but none would tangle with him when a title was on the line. That might have been a good call by all of them: Langford beat O'Brien and Gans, drew with Ketchel, and lost a close decision to Johnson, who refused a rematch and drew the color line on Langford once he had the world heavyweight championship.

Langford finally received recognition for his stellar career when he was one of the first boxers put into the International Boxing Hall of Fame in 1990.

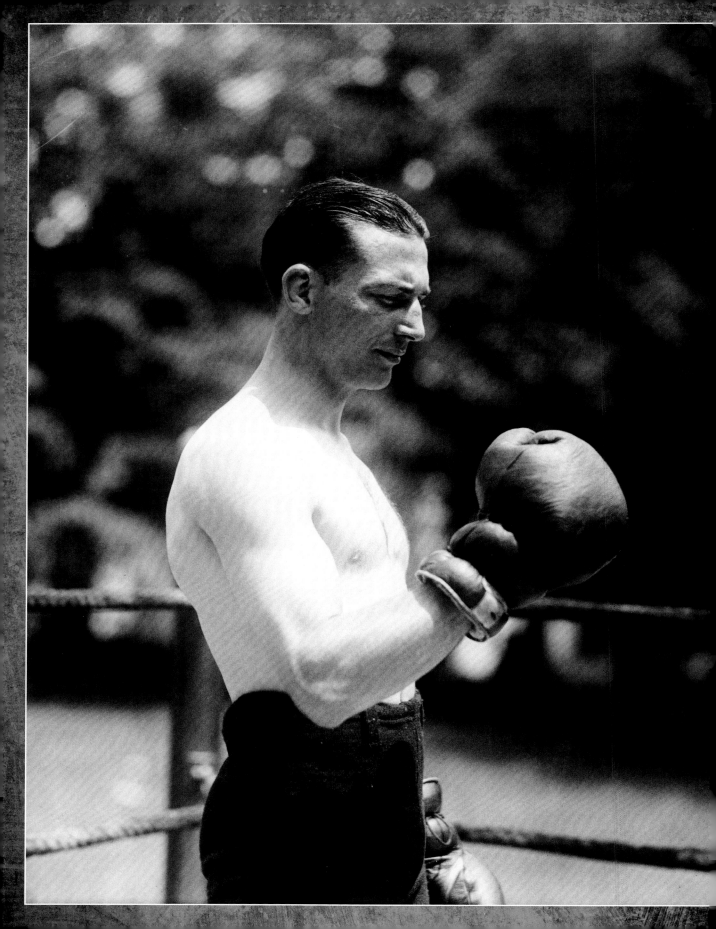

BENNY LEONARD

# ★★★★★ "THE GHETTO WIZARD" ★★★★★

NEW YORK, NY
BORN: April 7, 1896
DIED: April 18, 1947
HEIGHT: 5'5"
RECORD: 185–22–9, 3 NC (70 KOs)
TITLES WON: World Lightweight Champion
HALL OF FAME INDUCTION: 1990

They called Benny Leonard "The Ghetto Wizard," and what a wizard he was. So slick was he on fight night that some said he didn't even mess up his hair, Leonard made great fighters look ordinary and good fighters look like they weren't even supposed to be there in the first place.

Born Benjamin Leiner on the Lower East Side of New York City, Leonard grew up fighting on the streets to protect himself, so it was no surprise when he took to more conventional boxing. He turned pro in 1911 when he was just fifteen years old.

Fighting grown men taught the teenager the value of good defense. As his career progressed, he added some pop to his punches, making him a deadly fistic machine.

Getting to the top took some time, though. Leonard didn't win the lightweight title in 1917 until he had compiled more than a hundred fights. But in his second fight with Freddie Welsh, he was on top of his game, and he halted the champ in nine rounds.

Leonard held the title for more than six years. Although he lost a welterweight title challenge to Jack Britton in 1922, he was untouchable at 135 pounds. A fighter through and through, he retired on January 15, 1925, only at the request of his mother.

It was a rare happy ending for Leonard, but it wasn't to last. When the stock market crash of 1929 hit his bank account, he was forced to return to the ring. Still a step above the rest (although not as big a step as before), Leonard ran off twenty wins before fellow hall-of-famer Jimmy McLarnin stopped him in six rounds in October 1932.

Another boxer who died before his time, Leonard suffered a fatal heart attack while refereeing a boxing match in 1947, at just fifty-one years old.

SUGAR RAY LEONARD

PALMER PARK, MD
BORN: May 17, 1956
HEIGHT: 5'10"
RECORD: 36–3–1 (25 KOs)
TITLES WON: World Champion at Welterweight, Junior Middleweight, Middleweight, Super Middleweight, and Light Heavyweight; 1976 Olympic Gold Medalist
HALL OF FAME INDUCTION: 1997

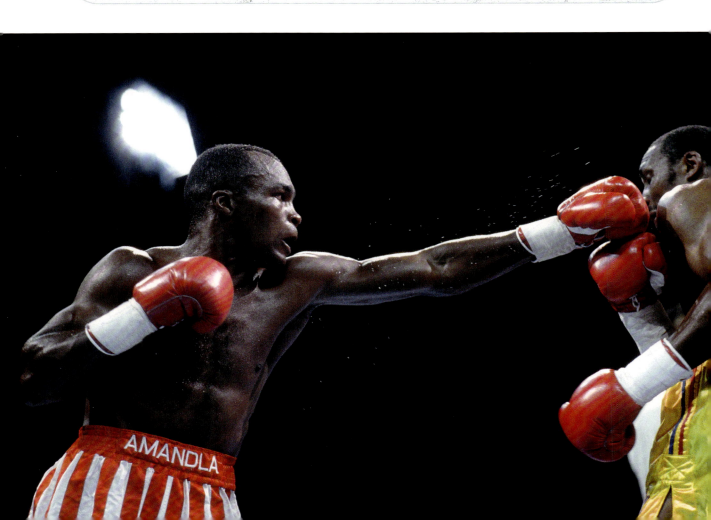

After winning Olympic gold in 1976, and taping his girlfriend's picture to his sock in the process, Sugar Ray Leonard was America's hero, the boy next door who did good. Add in matinee idol looks, charisma for days, and endless endorsements, and he was just the star boxing needed as Muhammad Ali's career came to an end.

But behind all that beat the heart of a true fighter. And if Leonard got you in trouble, he was going to finish you.

"When I hurt you, it was intuitive and it was instinctive, and especially if I saw a little blood, I went at you like Dracula," Leonard said. "And it's so funny because I'm so different than that person I was in the ring. I watch it now, and I say, 'Who the hell is that guy?' But I had that. I had that killer instinct."

Watch him fight, and you'll see it over and over again. Behind on points and with an eye rapidly swelling shut, Leonard came back to stop Thomas Hearns in the fourteenth round of their first fight in 1981. He put his superior boxing skills to the side to fight in the trenches with Roberto Durán in 1980's aptly titled "Brawl in Montreal." And then there was his willingness to come off a three-year layoff to move up to the middleweight division and face the feared Marvin Hagler in 1987, a night that saw Leonard upset the champ in a bout still talked about to this day.

This was the true Sugar Ray Leonard. And yes, winning titles in five different weight classes cemented his place in the International Hall of Fame and the history books, but for him it was all about the fights that mattered. He admitted that, if not for the other "Four Kings" (Durán, Hearns, and Hagler), we might not be talking about him the way we do today.

"It would be like most careers—satisfactory,"

Leonard said. "And as much as those guys needed me, I needed those guys. It's the same with Ali, Frazier, and Ken Norton. I needed those guys, and those guys brought the best out of me. And they made me the best fighter by me competing against them."

Despite being as humble as ever, Mr. Ray Charles Leonard agreed that it was a career well fought.

"I am totally satisfied, totally at peace," Leonard said. "During my time, I fought everyone who was out there."

LENNOX LEWIS

 "THE LION"

WEST HAM, LONDON, ENGLAND
BORN: September 2, 1965
HEIGHT: 6'5"
RECORD: 41–2–1 (32 KOs)
TITLES WON: World Heavyweight Champion; 1988 Olympic Gold Medalist
HALL OF FAME INDUCTION: 2009

Most people called Lennox Lewis "The Lion" during his fourteen-year professional career that saw him rule the heavyweight division for nearly a decade. The best moniker for the British-Canadian, though, is one he gave himself: The Pugilist Specialist.

Not only is it catchy, but it's accurate—and when he watches film of his fights, he sees that man at work.

"Classic," Lewis said when asked what runs through his mind when going down memory lane. "That man is the true pugilist specialist. And [promoter] Don King said I'm the 'Emperor of Boxing.' It's funny because, every time I watch them, I'm in tune and it's like I'm watching every shot like it's my first time. I always enjoy watching myself, and I'm definitely gonna bring out a DVD when all my fights come out with me commentating so you can actually hear what I was going through at that time, pre-fight or after the fight, and how I felt."

That would be a master class in boxing, for sure, considering how great Lewis was for so long. A two-time Olympian for Canada who struck gold in the 1988 games, Lewis's success on the amateur circuit translated smoothly to the pro game, where his size, power, and boxing ability kept him a step ahead of his peers.

That's not to say that there weren't hiccups. Lewis could get rocked, like he did against countryman Frank Bruno in 1993, and he suffered the loss of his heavyweight title twice via knockouts to Oliver McCall and Hasim Rahman.

But here's the thing: Lewis always came back in devastating fashion. He stopped both McCall and Rahman in rematches. Lewis felt he was at his best during the Rahman fight.

"That was a good night," he said. "We had a great Christmas after that."

Even his controversial 1999 draw with Evander Holyfield was avenged emphatically eight months later. As for the host of top-level opponents who challenged him during his reign (including Mike Tyson, David Tua, Andrew Golota, and Vitali Klitschko), Lewis dismissed them, too, in true pugilist specialist style.

"This is boxing, and we're supposed to be gladiators," he said. "People want to see you render the other guy unconscious."

SONNY LISTON

PHILADELPHIA, PA
BORN: May 8, 1932
DIED: December 30, 1970
HEIGHT: 6'1"
RECORD: 50–4 (39 KOs)
TITLES WON: World Heavyweight Champion
HALL OF FAME INDUCTION: 1991

During his "first" career, no one was more intimidating than George Foreman. He may have learned that part of the game from the original intimidator, Charles "Sonny" Liston, who was rarely seen with a smile on his face during the years he terrorized the heavyweight division.

It was no different with gloves on, and a young Foreman learned some valuable lessons from the Arkansas power puncher.

"I was just an amateur boxer," recalled Foreman. "I had won a little junior Golden Gloves tournament, and then I was given the opportunity to work with Sonny Liston. They said he needed some sparring, and I didn't know anything about sparring. All I knew was hit, hit, hit. And I really put it on him because I was so quick, and his trainer was telling him to take it easy on me. So he was trying to hold off and I was really cleaning him out. But then he hit me with a right hand and knocked me against the ropes, and Dick Sadler, who was his trainer then, said, 'Hold it, hold it, that's enough.' And I was glad."

Liston had that effect on opponents, and when he was on top of his game, no one could stop him. Boxing writer and manager Charles Farrell believes Liston was the greatest heavyweight of all time, which is quite the compliment when you consider that the boxer's troubles with the law almost derailed his promising career before it picked up steam.

But once it did, Liston used his jackhammer jab and thudding right hand to defeat the best boxers of the 1950s and '60s, including Cleveland Williams, Nino Valdes, Zora Folley, and Eddie Machen. In September 1962, the long-avoided Liston finally got his shot at the heavyweight title and needed just 2:06 to take it from Floyd Patterson. Ten months later, they met again, and Patterson was determined to avenge his loss and reclaim his title. This time around, it took Liston 2:10 to get the job done.

The fans and media didn't celebrate Liston, making him even more standoffish with both entities. But when a brash kid out of Louisville named Cassius Clay goaded him into a fight, the oddsmakers and boxing fans were in his corner.

Clay, who later changed his name to Muhammad Ali, was not to be denied: He forced Liston to quit in his corner after the sixth round on February 25, 1964. Fifteen months later, Ali halted Liston in the first round. Controversy swirled over both bouts, with some believing that Liston threw the fights, but no definitive answers came from those conspiracy theories.

The bottom line was that Ali was here to stay, and Liston's days as an elite heavyweight were over. He went 15–1 over his last sixteen fights, with his final victory being a ninth-round stoppage of Chuck Wepner on June 29, 1970. Nearly seven months later, Liston was found dead in his Las Vegas home. The official cause of death for the forty-year-old was a heroin overdose. Like so many things in his life, however, his final hours are shrouded in mystery, one that will likely never be solved.

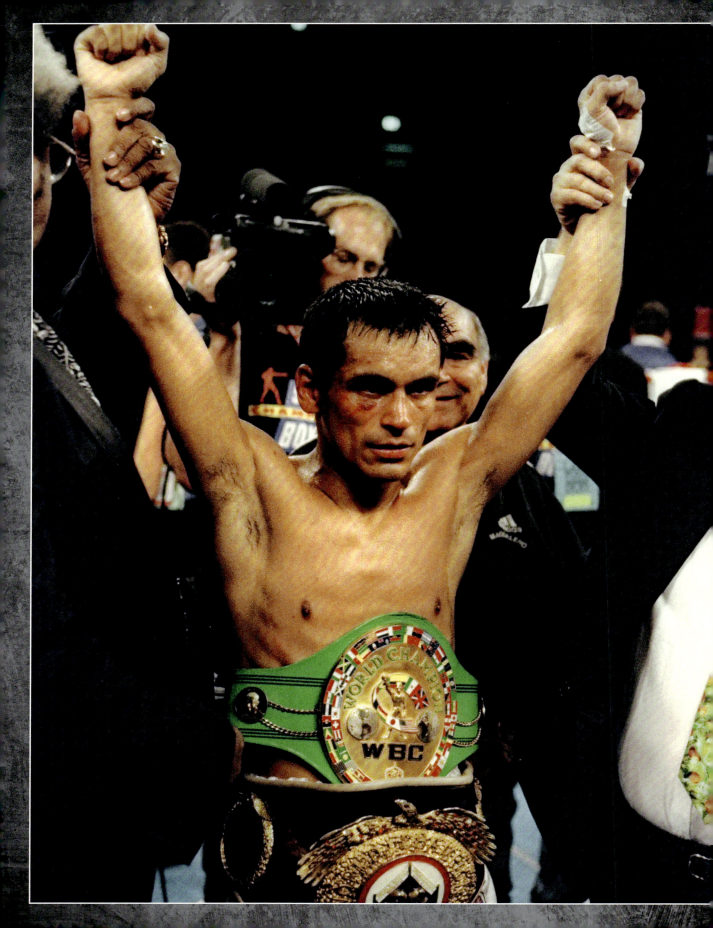

RICARDO LÓPEZ

✯✯✯✯✯ "EL FINITO" ✯✯✯✯✯

CUERNAVACA, MORELOS, MEXICO
BORN: July 25, 1966
HEIGHT: 5'5"
RECORD: 51–0–1 (38 KOs)
TITLES WON: World Champion at Mini Flyweight and Junior Flyweight
HALL OF FAME INDUCTION: 2007

No matter how you feel about Don King and his impact on the sport, the one thing you can always say about the loquacious and controversial promoter is that he always gave fans their money's worth.

In King's heyday, fight cards started in the afternoon and ran into the night, featuring not just high-profile headliners, but also experienced contenders, rising stars, and champions who wouldn't get significant exposure in any other format.

Enter Ricardo López. Featured on some of the biggest pay-per-view cards King ever promoted, the five-foot-five Mexican warrior thrilled fans with his technical brilliance and the power that earned him the nickname "Finito." He guaranteed that fans would be in their seat or in front of their television when he was scheduled to fight.

López never disappointed them, either, as he compiled a 51–0–1 career record while dominating two weight classes from 1990 until his 2002 retirement. That's quite a long time to not just stay unbeaten, but also face the best in the world night in and night out as a champion and also successfully defend his WBC minimumweight (105 pounds) title twenty-two times.

The last two may have been the most special, as López faced the only man to truly test him: Rosendo Álvarez. In their first fight in March 1998, a technical draw produced the only blemish on López's record. Eight months later, they met again, this time with López taking a close split-decision victory.

Within a year, López had moved up to 108 pounds and beat Will Grigsby for a new title, which he defended twice. He retired after a knockout of Zolani Petelo in 2001.

TOMMY LOUGHRAN

 "THE PHILLY PHANTOM"

PHILADELPHIA, PA
BORN: November 29, 1902
DIED: July 7, 1982
HEIGHT: 5'11½"
RECORD: 90–25–10, 1 NC (14 KOs)
TITLES WON: World Light Heavyweight Champion
HALL OF FAME INDUCTION: 1991

Tommy "The Philly Phantom" Loughran never made a lot of noise, but in a professional career that lasted nearly two decades, he fought a strength of schedule that would have scared most of his peers. It spoke volumes about the Philadelphia native's warrior spirit.

To make matters more difficult, oft-injured hands forced him to rely on pure boxing, not brawling, to secure his ninety wins. Loughran, a light heavyweight champion from 1927 to 1929 who never lost his belt in the ring, wasn't afraid to face bigger opposition, either—most notably, six-foot-six, 270-pound Primo Carnera, whom he challenged for the world heavyweight title in 1934.

Loughran lost that bout to Carnera, but among the notable heavyweights he defeated over the years were Max Baer, Jim Braddock, Arturo Godoy, Jack Sharkey, King Levinsky, and Ernie Schaaf. That's three world champions right there. Impressive, but when he wasn't giving up size and strength to his foes, Loughran was at his best, and the record proves it:

He defeated Mickey Walker, Jimmy Slattery, Mike McTigue, Georges Carpentier, and Young Stribling. He even fought Gene Tunney and engaged in a six-fight series with Harry Greb.

Going over that resume reminds us how good Loughran was and how fearless he was in facing all comers. Sadly, without the flash of some of his peers and the recognition that higher-profile athletes received in that era, Loughran was largely forgotten. He faded away until his 1991 induction into the International Boxing Hall of Fame reminded the world that "The Philly Phantom" was a legitimate great in the boxing ring.

JOE LOUIS

 "THE BROWN BOMBER"

DETROIT, MI
BORN: May 13, 1914
DIED: April 12, 1981
HEIGHT: 6'1½"
RECORD: 66–3 (52 KOs)
TITLES WON: World Heavyweight Champion
HALL OF FAME INDUCTION: 1990

Most boxing careers don't last twelve years. Joe Louis was heavyweight champion for twelve years, making twenty-five successful title defenses. His record still stands today across all divisions, more than seventy-five years after he set it.

That's a mic drop.

We could walk away now and know why he's on this list, but we won't. So many facets to Louis's life made him a fascinating figure whose impact on boxing—and the world—will never be forgotten.

Remember, there was still a color line in sports when Louis was making his way up the ladder. In heavyweight boxing, it was even worse for Black fighters because the powers-that-be didn't want a repeat of what had happened when Jack Johnson became champion and thumbed his nose at racists and the power brokers in the game. Louis's talent was undeniable, but his managers gave him a list of things he couldn't do if he wanted to succeed, including not having his picture taken with a white woman.

Sad, but true.

Louis stuck to the list and kept knocking out opponents, including former world champions Primo Carnera and Max Baer, before a brief hiccup, when he was stopped by Max Schmeling in 1936. Undeterred by his first pro loss, he made a quick return to prominence and got a shot at champion Jim Braddock in June 1937. Louis was floored early in the fight, but he came back and knocked out Braddock in the eighth round. The world had a new heavyweight champion.

A busy champ, Louis took on and beat all comers, most notably Schmeling in a 1938 rematch at Yankee Stadium that stopped the world. With World War II just around the corner, American hero Louis, looking to avenge his only loss, took no

mercy on Germany's Schmeling, knocking him out in two minutes and four seconds.

Then it was back to less political action in the ring. The title defenses piled up, interrupted only by his service with the US Army in World War II. When Louis returned to the ring in 1946, he had lost a step, as evidenced by a controversial decision win over Jersey Joe Walcott. Louis knocked out Walcott in the rematch and retired, relinquishing his title.

However, he returned in 1950 for a final chance to challenge the best of the best in Ezzard Charles and Rocky Marciano. He didn't defeat either, but he left the sport a champion forever, both in and out of the ring.

RAY MANCINI

 "BOOM BOOM"

YOUNGSTOWN, OH
BORN: March 4, 1961
HEIGHT: 5'4½"
RECORD: 29–5 (23 KOs)
TITLES WON: World Lightweight Champion
HALL OF FAME INDUCTION: 2015

In what was perhaps boxing's last golden age in the 1980s, Ray "Boom Boom" Mancini was every mother's son—but he will always be remembered as Lenny's boy. Mancini's action-packed style and affable personality would have made him a star in any era, but it was the story of his relationship with his father that captivated a nation.

Lenny Mancini was a lightweight contender who was closing in on a title shot before World War II intervened. Mancini was wounded in battle in 1944, and although he received a Purple Heart, he was never able to get the shot at a championship that had once seemed inevitable.

His son Ray thus made it his mission to get the title his father had never gotten to fight for. With CBS on board to air Mancini's journey on free network television, young "Boom Boom" became a star.

"[Manager] Dave Wolf knew how to sell the story of me and my father," said Mancini. "But here's the difference—it was a real story. The old saying in marketing is that you sell the sizzle, not the steak. But you've gotta have a good piece of steak because you only get one shot. And when people say, 'Television made you,' there's no dispute about that, but here's the rub—if I'm a losing fighter, then what does it mean? I could fight a little bit, too."

More than a little bit, as it turned out. The dream may have been delayed when Mancini was stopped in the fourteenth round by Alexis Argüello in a gritty 1981 title bout, but seven months later, the Youngstown, Ohio native won the title for his dad with a first-round stoppage of Arturo Frias.

Fans didn't pull back after seeing Mancini's dream fulfilled. His following only grew as he defended his title against Ernesto España in front of his loyal Ohio fans. Yet with his momentum picking up even more speed, a brutal war with South Korea's Duk Koo Kim

on November 13, 1982 changed everything.

On paper, Mancini won an epic championship bout knocking out the courageous Kim in the fourteenth round. Unfortunately, Kim died from injuries five days later. The twenty-one-year-old Mancini was understandably shattered by this turn of events, especially followed by the suicides of Kim's mother and referee Richard Green. The WBC, which sanctioned the fight, shortened the length of championship fights from fifteen to twelve rounds, and the marketing machine that lined up to get on the Mancini bandwagon pulled back after the tragedy.

Despite this, Mancini fought on and had a successful career. He defended his title twice more before he lost it to Livingstone Bramble in 1984, while also engaging in high-profile bouts with Héctor Camacho and Greg Haugen en route to a 2015 International Boxing Hall of Fame induction.

ROCKY MARCIANO

 **"THE BROCKTON BLOCKBUSTER"**

BROCKTON, MA
BORN: September 1, 1923
DIED: August 31, 1969
HEIGHT: 5'10"
RECORD: 49–0 (43 KOs)
TITLES WON: World Heavyweight Champion
HALL OF FAME INDUCTION: 1990

It's funny what sticks in the head of an impressionable youth. For years, in a household where it was God, country, and Rocky Marciano (not necessarily in that order), my father would tell me of the time when "The Rock" hit Roland LaStarza so often and so hard in the arms during their second bout in 1953 that he broke blood vessels. The result? The challenger to the heavyweight championship, who gave Marciano a tough go in their first fight three years earlier, eventually couldn't lift his arms to defend his head, leading to an eleventh-round TKO victory for the pride of Brockton, Massachusetts.

Marciano, just three weeks removed from his thirtieth birthday, fought just four more times, beating Ezzard Charles (twice), Don Cockell, and Archie Moore before retiring with a perfect 49–0 record at the age of thirty-two. It was the perfect—and rarest—example of an athlete leaving on top, his unbeaten slate untouched for decades.

Not bad for an aspiring baseball catcher who made it through three weeks of a tryout with a Chicago Cubs farm team before he was cut. But boxing, not baseball, was Marciano's ticket. After a fairly unimpressive amateur career, he turned pro in 1947. He did nothing but win, but he had his doubters: After the Brockton native's win over Gino Buonvino in 1950, the *Boston Traveler*'s Arthur Siegel wrote that Marciano was "nothing more than a good club fighter."

Marciano was unconcerned with such criticism, and he wanted to test himself against the division's elite. His brother Lou "Sonny" Marciano told me, "He wanted so much to look good because it was the time

when he was getting into the big time. He had great confidence in his ability, and he was so determined and trained so hard that he reached a point where he knew that he was ready and that he would definitely go all the way."

In the year following the Buonvino bout, Marciano fought—and won—seven times.

Then in October 1951, he knocked out his hero, Joe Louis, in the eighth round. It was an emotional moment for Marciano, who cried in his locker room after the fight, but it was also the victory that put him on the world map as a future title challenger.

On September 23, 1952, he got his shot and made the most of it, rising from the canvas to score one of the most epic knockouts in boxing history against Jersey Joe Walcott in the thirteenth round.

The "good club fighter" was now the heavyweight champion of the world.

Marciano, a relentless pressure fighter with thudding power, heart for days, and underrated defensive skills, successfully defended his crown six times before retiring with a win. That's all Rocky Marciano knew. And he told Lou as much when his brother asked his plans for upcoming fights.

"Don't ever question what I'm gonna do," said "The Rock." "I'm gonna win."

JUAN MANUEL MÁRQUEZ

 "DINAMITA"

MEXICO CITY, MEXICO
BORN: August 23, 1973
HEIGHT: 5′7″
RECORD: 56–7–1 (40 KOs)
TITLES WON: World Champion at Featherweight, Junior Lightweight, and Lightweight
HALL OF FAME INDUCTION: 2020

For the longest time, Juan Manuel Márquez was the odd man out. The Mexico City native was an elite featherweight, racing out to a 39–2 record before stopping Manuel Medina in seven rounds to win the IBF world title in February 2003. When it came to the biggest stars to emerge from his native country, though, he seemed to occupy the shadows of Marco Antonio Barrera and Erik Morales.

Márquez was just as talented as his countrymen, but he wasn't getting the same adulation or big fight opportunities. But he was patient.

"Life without problems is no life," Márquez said. "Being happy all the time, I don't consider that life, and it's impossible. You have to learn from the negative experiences and try to be happy. There's nothing else you can do. I'm positive, and I'm gonna keep boxing because it gives me a lot of satisfaction. Maybe it hasn't given me the money I was expecting, but I have a family, I got what I need, and there are a lot of things to come."

Like Manny Pacquiao. Finally faced with a dance partner capable of taking his notoriety and fight game to the next level, Márquez waged war with Pacquiao four times, each time bigger than the last. "Dinamita" got the last word with an emphatic knockout of the Filipino icon in their fourth fight in 2011.

By then, Márquez had won three divisional world titles; beaten Barrera; faced Floyd Mayweather Jr., Timothy Bradley, and Juan Díaz; and finally gotten his due from his nation and the world.

CHRISTY MARTIN

 "THE COAL MINER'S DAUGHTER"

MULLENS, WV
BORN: June 12, 1968
HEIGHT: 5'4½"
RECORD: 49–7–3 (31 KOs)
TITLES WON: World Junior Middleweight Champion
HALL OF FAME INDUCTION: 2020

No one intimidated Christy Martin—except Marvin Hagler. When Martin was invited to be the Grand Marshal of the International Boxing Hall of Fame's Parade of Champions in 1996, she almost turned down the offer because she was likely to run into one of her fistic idols.

But she went, and at the end of the weekend, there was Marvelous Marvin, who greeted Martin with pure, blunt honesty.

"You have a really good left hook."

He was right, which was evident during a year in which Martin won her biggest fight to date against Deirdre Gogarty three months earlier and was featured on the cover of Sports Illustrated (the first and only female boxer to receive the honor). A compliment from Hagler? That was the icing on the cake.

"That's the kind of respect and love I have for boxing, for the hall of fame, for the legends," said Martin, who joined those legends in 2020 as part of the first class of women to be inducted into boxing's hall of the greats. It was a long time coming for the ladies—and if not for Martin, those doors still might be closed.

"The Coal Miner's Daughter" was the first woman to gain mainstream media exposure due to her appearance on Don King–promoted undercards, and fans fell in love with a fighter who broke all the stereotypes of what a female boxer was supposed to be. She threw that left hook with abandon, she turned boxing matches into fights, and her toughness was unmatched. And she wasn't doing it against stiffs: She fought elite foes such as Laura Serrano, Isra Girgrah, Marcela Acuña, Sumya Anani, Belinda Laracuente, Kathy Collins, and her future wife, Lisa Holewyne.

But her toughness was put to the test outside the ring when her then-husband and longtime trainer and

manager, Jim Martin, attempted to kill her in 2010. Christy survived; and Jim was convicted and sentenced to twenty-five years in prison for the attack.

Martin went on to become an advocate for domestic abuse survivors, showing that she was well equipped for another fight in retirement. It was just another reason why people say fighters are born, not made, and West Virginia's finest was born for this.

"I simply wanted to be a fighter," she said. "I just wanted to fit in. I didn't want everybody to say, 'Oh wow, Christy is a good woman fighter.' I wanted them to say, 'Wow, Christy's a good fighter.'"

FLOYD MAYWEATHER JR.

 "MONEY"

GRAND RAPIDS, MI
BORN: February 24, 1977
HEIGHT: 5'8"
RECORD: 50–0 (27 KOs)
TITLES WON: World Champion at Junior Lightweight, Lightweight, Junior Welterweight, Welterweight, and Junior Middleweight
HALL OF FAME INDUCTION: 2021

I don't know if Leonard Ellerbe ever got used to the 4 a.m. phone calls. "You never have to push him to do anything," said the longtime friend of Floyd Mayweather Jr. and former CEO of Mayweather Promotions. "He's the one calling me at four in the morning, 'Come on, I'm ready to go.' And that's when we're not training for a fight."

Those early morning roadwork sessions became the stuff of legend. Although people paid big bucks to see Mayweather compete on fight night, he could have gotten an equal amount of cash from fans to watch him train. There was the epic mitt work with his uncle Roger, sparring rounds that often went up to fifteen minutes, and an attention to detail that made him the best boxer of his era.

For all the glitz and glamour and the "Money" Mayweather persona, the Grand Rapids native was always the hardest worker in the room.

A bronze medalist in the 1996 Olympics, Mayweather came from a fighting family that included his father, Floyd Sr., and uncles Roger and Jeff. Mayweather's loss to Serafim Todorov in the Atlanta games was the last time he ever lost in the ring. As a professional, Mayweather posted a perfect 50–0 record that saw him win world titles in five weight classes. Among the elite fighters Mayweather defeated were Shane Mosley, Ricky Hatton, Manny Pacquiao, "Canelo" Álvarez, Miguel Cotto, José Luis Castillo, Diego Corrales, Oscar De La Hoya, Zab Judah, Arturo Gatti, and Genaro Hernández. Except for Castillo and Mosley, no one even tested him.

"Hard work, dedication" was Mayweather's mantra—and it made him one of the best ever.

"Every day, I tell myself I'm a winner," he said. "I was born to be a winner at life. Not just in the ring, but I was born to be a winner. So whatever I do, I try to give it 100 percent and I try to push my limit."

TERRY McGOVERN

"TERRIBLE"

BROOKLYN, NY
BORN: March 9, 1880
DIED: February 22, 1918
HEIGHT: 5'3"
RECORD: 60–4–3, 1 NC (45 KOs)
TITLES WON: World Bantamweight and Featherweight Champion
HALL OF FAME INDUCTION: 1990

To put it succinctly, "Terrible" Terry McGovern was not a practitioner of the sweet science. He showed up for a fistfight, and if an opponent wasn't ready for that, they would get run over—even if fighters at the turn of the century were trying to introduce a more refined, technique-based style to what just a few years earlier was an outlaw sport.

That aggressive, brawling style led the small but powerful McGovern to world championships at bantamweight and featherweight and eventually to a place in the International Boxing Hall of Fame in 1990.

McGovern didn't pay any mind to the politics or honors, though. He knew that winning fights would help his family financially, so he did whatever it took to win them. And win he did, even though he competed at a time when the records of top-level fighters weren't so glossy. That McGovern won sixty of his sixty-eight pro fights indicates how good he was.

A first-round finish of Pedlar Palmer in 1899 earned McGovern the bantamweight title, and he defeated George Dixon in 1900 to take the featherweight championship. He even beat lightweight champion Frank Erne in 1900, but the bout was considered to be of the nontitle variety.

McGovern got knocked out by Young Corbett II in 1903 and lost his featherweight crown, but he never lost his bantamweight title in the ring. He fought on until 1906, and he died of pneumonia and Bright's disease at age thirty-seven on February 22, 1918.

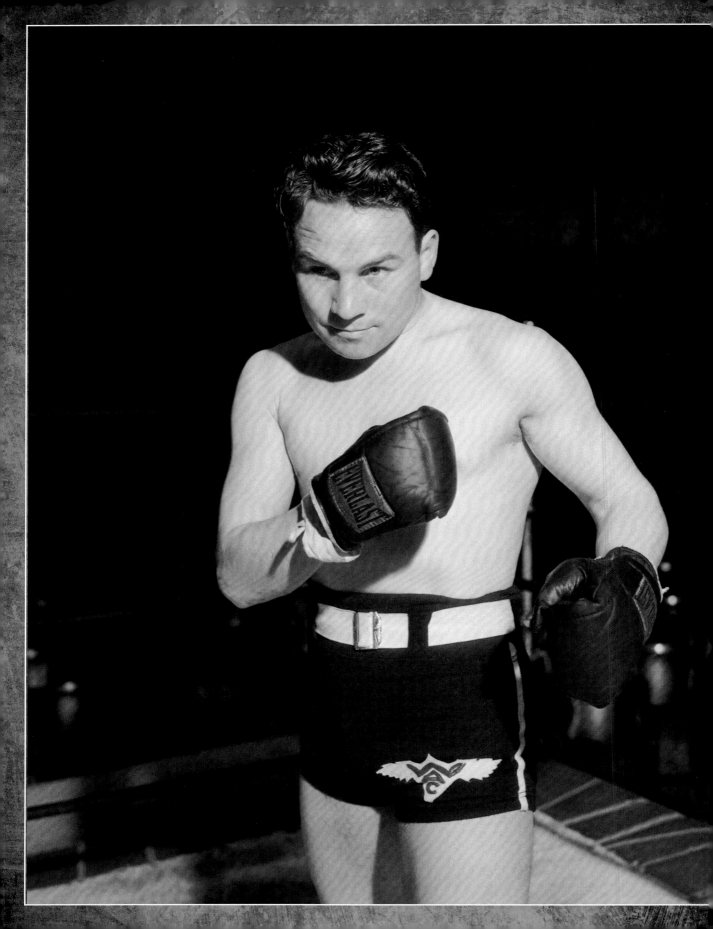

JIMMY McLARNIN

 "BABY FACE"

HILLSBOROUGH, NORTHERN IRELAND
BORN: December 19, 1907
DIED: October 28, 2004
HEIGHT: 5'6"
RECORD: 55–11–3 (21 KOs)
TITLES WON: World Welterweight Champion
HALL OF FAME INDUCTION: 1991

Happy endings in boxing are rare, but Jimmy McLarnin created one for himself. Retiring in 1936 at the age of twenty-nine, the Northern Ireland native was apparently still in his prime, considering that his last two fights were wins over Tony Canzoneri and Lou Ambers. McLarnin walked away and never returned, living a long and productive life with his wife of fifty years, Lillian, before he died in 2004 at the age of ninety-six.

McLarnin, a father of four, also lived long enough to see himself get a place in the International Boxing Hall of Fame in 1991. That was a well-deserved honor for someone who not only ruled the welterweight division, but also fought challengers from practically all weight classes, including Pancho Villa, Fidel LaBarba, Sammy Mandell, Benny Leonard, and the aforementioned Canzoneri and Ambers.

But the skilled boxer-puncher did his best work as a welterweight, and he won the world title in 1933 by knocking out Young Corbett III in a single round. A year after his title-winning effort, McLarnin began a memorable three-fight series with Barney Ross that drew sixty thousand people to their first meeting at the Madison Square Garden Bowl in Long Island City. He lost his title in their first bout, regained it in their middle fight, and then lost it once more in 1935. This trilogy captivated fight fans and forever linked the careers of both men.

A year and a half after that final showdown with Ross, McLarnin left the proverbial building, never to return. Kudos to him for being one of the rare fighters to leave the sport on top with still more to give. It was proof positive that one of the smartest boxers inside the ropes was just as smart outside them.

CARLOS MONZÓN

 "ESCOPETA"

SANTA FE, ARGENTINA
BORN: August 7, 1942
DIED: January 8, 1995
HEIGHT: 5'11"
RECORD: 87–3–9, 1 NC (59 KOs)
TITLES WON: World Middleweight Champion
HALL OF FAME INDUCTION: 1990

It's always difficult to write about a boxer who (A) isn't around to defend himself and (B) was a convicted murderer.

That was Carlos Monzón, who died in a car crash in 1995 during a furlough from prison, where he was serving an eleven-year sentence for killing the mother of his son, Alicia Muñiz, in 1988.

So we've established that, as a human being, Monzón wasn't a good one. In the ring, however, he was a master, able to harness his demons long enough to become one of the greatest middleweights in boxing history.

Monzón posted an 87-3-9, 1 NC record during his career. It's important to point out that his three losses all came before he had compiled twenty fights, and he avenged all of them. A lot of time passed before he made it to a world title—seventy-nine fights, to be exact—but when he traveled to Roma, Italy, to face local hero Nino Benvenuti on November 7, 1970, Monzón was ready: He made the most of that opportunity and stopped his foe in the twelfth round of *The Ring* magazine's Fight of the Year.

The rematch six months later wasn't close, and of Monzón's fourteen title defenses, only Emile Griffith and Rodrigo Valdes truly tested him. Considering that the Argentinean successfully defended his crown against Bennie Briscoe, José Nápoles, Tony Licata, and Tony Mundine, that's saying something. It proves that, for all his post-boxing issues, Monzón was a special fighter.

ARCHIE MOORE

 "THE OLD MONGOOSE"

BENOIT, MS
BORN: December 13, 1913
DIED: December 9, 1998
HEIGHT: 5'11"
RECORD: 186–23–10, 1 NC (132 KOs)
TITLES WON: World Light Heavyweight Champion
HALL OF FAME INDUCTION: 1990

For nearly three decades, Archie Moore's commitment to excellence kept him at the top of the boxing world. With a distinct style and an unparalleled power that saw him score a record 132 knockouts, he became the longest-reigning light heavyweight champion in history.

Moore reigned atop the 175-pound weight class for ten years, characterized by his ever-present knockout power, pristine defense, and sublime fight IQ. It's no wonder he's considered not just one of the best light heavyweights ever, but one of the best, pound for pound, of all time.

For the reasons just mentioned, Moore was ducked for a long time before he got a world title shot—seventeen years, to be exact. When he got his chance to face light heavyweight champion Joey Maxim in December 1952, the thirty-nine-year-old Moore was ready: He decisioned Maxim over fifteen rounds.

No fighter nearing forty years of age, even one of Moore's caliber, would be expected to hold a title for too long, but "The Old Mongoose" was something special: He reigned for ten years and never lost his title in the ring.

Chief among his memorable title defenses was his 1958 war with Yvon Durelle. Dropped four times, Moore got up each time and scored four knockdowns of his own en route to an eleventh-round knockout win. He also fought for the heavyweight title twice, losing to Rocky Marciano (whom he knocked down) and Floyd Patterson. In one of his final fights, he was stopped by a young Cassius Clay.

It was quite a career. Moore went on to stay in the game as a trainer, most notably with George Foreman.

ERIK MORALES

"EL TERRIBLE"

TIJUANA, MEXICO
BORN: September 1, 1976
HEIGHT: 5'8"
RECORD: 52–9 (36 KOs)
TITLES WON: World Champion at Junior Featherweight, Featherweight, Junior Lightweight, and Junior Welterweight
HALL OF FAME INDUCTION: 2018

Time had not healed all wounds for Erik Morales. In thirty-six rounds from 2000 to 2004, "El Terrible" and Marco Antonio Barrera engaged in a Mexican Civil War that was anything but civil. Whether brawling at press conferences or in the ring, these two didn't like each other one bit.

Even a year after their final bout with each other, which left Barrera with a 2–1 edge, Morales was still salty about his rival. That was unfortunate because you always wanted to picture the pair as old men sitting on the porch sharing a beer. That's how connected Morales and Barrera will always be, even though the Tijuana native did plenty outside their classic trilogy.

Fifty-two wins, thirty-six knockouts, and a place in the history books as the first Mexican to win world titles in four weight classes earned him a place in the International Boxing Hall of Fame in 2018.

But what made Morales special was who he beat and how he did it. Aggressive, accurate, and powerful, the lanky Morales made opponents fight. If they didn't, they got wiped out. If they did, they were in for the toughest night of their careers.

In addition to Barrera and Zaragoza, Morales vanquished elite foes that included Junior Jones, Wayne McCullough, Kevin Kelley, Paulie Ayala, and Manny Pacquiao. He even took a world title against Pablo César Cano in 2011, eighteen years after his pro debut, forever establishing his bona fides.

But in a plot twist, retirement not only mellowed Morales: it also put him next to Barrera as FOX Deportes commentators. Did the ice thaw?

"When we were young, we did what we had to do," said Morales. "It was a sporting rivalry that, unfortunately, got personal, but in the end, what people remember us for are those great fights that we gave to the sport. Now,

since then, we've been able to come together."

It was a surprising turn of events, but Morales, who could switch styles upon command in the ring, depending on the moment, was used to surprising both fight fans and opponents, who didn't know whether they were in a boxing match or a brawl. That mastery in the ring was the epitome of greatness from one of Mexico's finest.

SHANE MOSLEY

 "SUGAR"

POMONA, CA
BORN: September 7, 1971
HEIGHT: 5'9"
RECORD: 49–10–1, 1 NC (41 KOs)
TITLES WON: World Champion at Lightweight, Welterweight, and Junior Middleweight
HALL OF FAME INDUCTION: 2020

The year was 1998. Shane Mosley was the lightweight champion of the world. He was unbeaten and seemingly unbeatable. Mosley was so good that it looked like he would reign forever. But that doesn't happen in boxing, and he was smart enough to know it. He told me that he knew someone would have his number one day.

He was right, but more often than not, "Sugar" Shane was the one handing out Ls, thanks in no small part to a style he called "power boxing."

"We fight at a certain level where, if the guy can't keep up to the tempo that I'm at, then he's going to fall to the wayside, and he's gonna get knocked out or stopped," said Mosley. "And then if he maintains that, then I just step it up a step higher and go to the next level. It's basically boxing real hard. Throwing a lot of crisp, sharp punches hard and fast."

It sounds simple, if a bit taxing, but that style, perfected over twenty-three years in the pro ring, thrilled fans. It also earned the Pomona native three divisional world titles and landed him a spot in the International Boxing Hall of Fame's Class of 2020.

Mosley had it all in the ring: speed, power, combination punching, and heart, making him a worthy successor to Sugar Ray Robinson and Sugar Ray Leonard. But Mosley was no imitator—he was his own man. As dominant as he was at 135 pounds, he fought largely under the radar until he moved up to the welterweight division, where he shook up the boxing world in 2000 with a win over "The Golden Boy," Oscar De La Hoya.

Three title defenses followed before he lost to the boxer who had his number—Vernon Forrest. Of Mosley's ten losses, two came to Forrest and two came to Winky Wright. But there were enough good times in victory and defeat against Ricardo Mayorga, Floyd Mayweather Jr., Antonio Margarito, "Canelo" Álvarez, Manny Pacquiao, Fernando Vargas, and Miguel Cotto to clearly establish Mosley as one of the best of his era.

AZUMAH NELSON

★★★★★ "THE PROFESSOR" ★★★★★

ACCRA, GHANA
BORN: July 19, 1958
HEIGHT: 5'5"
RECORD: 39–6–2 (28 KOs)
TITLES WON: World Champion at Featherweight and Junior Lightweight
HALL OF FAME INDUCTION: 2004

The small village of Bukom in the suburbs of Accra, Ghana, is known throughout the boxing world for producing a seemingly endless stream of elite boxers and world champions.

It's a great story, considering that Bukom is far from a boxing hub such as Las Vegas, New York City, or Los Angeles. Yet for all the champions who came from the small gym, none was greater than Azumah Nelson.

Nicknamed "The Professor," Nelson put on master classes in the ring whenever he was called to perform, even when, at just 13–0 as a pro, he was asked to fly to New York to face WBC featherweight champ Salvador Sánchez on just two weeks' notice on July 21, 1982.

Relatively unknown outside Africa, Nelson changed that status over fifteen rounds with Sánchez. He lost a decision to the Mexican great (who, sadly, died in a car crash three weeks after the bout), but Nelson had made a name for himself and became a fighter to watch.

Nelson took advantage of his newfound notoriety, parlaying six wins into another world title fight, this time against Puerto Rican star Wilfredo Gómez. But it was Nelson's fists that did the talking, as he knocked out "Bazooka" in the eleventh round to win the WBC featherweight crown.

Six successful title defenses followed before "The Professor" moved to the junior lightweight division and won a second championship by decisioning Mario Martínez on February 29, 1988. An attempt to win another belt at 135 pounds fell short when he was beaten by Pernell Whitaker, but Nelson returned to 130 and continued to rule with an iron fist, with only draws against Jeff Fenech and Jesse James Leija marring his winning streak.

A loss to Leija in their 1994 rematch ended Nelson's reign at age thirty-six. He went into retirement just a few years later as a hall-of-famer and a revered ambassador for boxing, both in Africa and around the globe.

PHILADELPHIA JACK O'BRIEN

PHILADELPHIA, PA
BORN: January 17, 1878
DIED: November 12, 1942
HEIGHT: 5'10"
RECORD: 147–16–24, 5 NC (55 KOs)
TITLES WON: World Light Heavyweight Champion
HALL OF FAME INDUCTION: 1994

Long considered to be the dean of American boxing writers, A.J. Liebling could make or break a career with one of his columns in *The New Yorker*. So when he wrote five thousand words on Philadelphia Jack O'Brien in his book *Back Where I Came From*, it was a big deal for someone who wasn't a baseball superstar or a heavyweight champion, especially because the man born James Francis Hagan was already retired.

O'Brien certainly was a big deal, thanks to nearly two hundred fights and a brief reign as the world light heavyweight champion. His impact outside the ring was just as notable. Newspapers chronicled his every move, making him a legitimate star at the end of the 1800s and into the early 1900s.

What truly captivated everyone who saw him, though, is that, in a sport filled with crude brawlers, O'Brien was a true sweet scientist. A technical marvel, he used brains instead of brawn to defeat opponents such as Barbados Joe Walcott, Marvin Hart, and Young Peter Jackson.

In 1905, O'Brien stamped his name on the world boxing map with a thirteenth-round stoppage of former heavyweight champion Bob Fitzsimmons to win the light heavyweight title. Considering that he beat "Ruby Robert" and future heavyweight champ Tommy Burns, O'Brien decided—like so many 175-pound titlists after him—to chase after gold in the sport's glamour division.

On his quest for the heavyweight crown (remember, there was only one champion back then, not four in each division), O'Brien met Burns twice more and even clashed with middleweight champion Stanley Ketchel and future Joe Louis trainer Jack Blackburn.

O'Brien finally met champion Jack Johnson on May 19, 1909. Although their bout was ruled a draw by local newspapers, many believed that O'Brien outboxed his foe, who outweighed him by more than forty pounds.

That was as close as O'Brien got to a heavyweight title, and he retired in 1912. He didn't go out as a heavyweight champion, but being considered an all-time great at light heavyweight was good enough for this hall-of-famer to earn his place in the annals of boxing history.

RUBÉN OLIVARES

 "EL PÚAS"

MEXICO CITY, MEXICO
BORN: January 14, 1947
HEIGHT: 5'5½"
RECORD: 89–13–3 (79 KOs)
TITLES WON: World Champion at Bantamweight and Featherweight

For someone whose prime saw him compete at 118 pounds, Rubén Olivares could pack a punch.

How much of a punch? Try an 89 percent knockout rate that was compiled not with thirty wins, but eighty-nine over a twenty-three-year career. With that much explosiveness, it's no surprise that "Rockabye Rubén" was a star both in his native Mexico and in Southern California, where he fought many of his most memorable bouts with his take-no-prisoners style.

Olivares turned pro in 1965 and quickly established himself on the local Mexican fight circuit, winning his first twenty-four bouts by knockout. By mid-1969, he sported a remarkable 52–0–1 record with fifty knockouts and was matched up with bantamweight champion Lionel Rose at The Forum in Inglewood, California. It took Olivares just five rounds to take the title, becoming the first to knock Rose out in the process.

A little more than a year later, on October 16, 1970, Olivares lost for the first time. He was stopped by Chucho Castillo, whom he had decisioned just ten months earlier. They met again in early 1971, and Olivares took back his title by a fifteen-round unanimous decision.

After losing the belt a second time, this time to Rafael Herrera, Olivares moved to the featherweight division, where the power remained. He came through with a seventh-round knockout of Zensuke Utagawa for the WBA title in his sixteenth appearance at The Forum. Later that year, Olivares lost to a hungry former sparring partner named Alexis Argüello, who described a prefight exchange with the champion.

"I sparred with Rubén Olivares when he came to fight Yambito Blanco," Argüello recalled. "And I said that if I want to learn, I have to spar with this world champion. I didn't even tell my trainer that I was doing it, but I had to go. And he beat the living crap out of me. He put a black eye on me. That was in 1971. And then I went to fight him in 1974, and I

asked him, 'Rubén, do you remember when you put a black eye on me?' And he said, 'Hey kid, I don't remember you, but I'm gonna send you home early. I don't want to punish you. That's okay kid, I'll take care of you really early. That way you don't suffer.' I said, 'Are you kidding me? I came here to do something for my country, buddy. Don't take it too lightly. I'm here to battle it out. Whatever's going to happen, I respect you. I'm just trying to remind you about what you did when I was a kid. But the best will win tonight, buddy.' I remember I said that."

Argüello won that battle, but Olivares continued to fight and thrill fans, ultimately landing in the International Boxing Hall of Fame in 1991.

MANUEL ORTIZ

CORONA, CA
BORN: July 2, 1916
DIED: May 31, 1970
HEIGHT: 5'4"
RECORD: 99–28–3 (53 KOs)
TITLES WON: World Bantamweight Champion
HALL OF FAME INDUCTION: 1996

In a bantamweight division that didn't get much national notice, Manuel Ortiz nonetheless made his mark as an elite boxer. In the three decades he fought, from the 1930s to the 1950s, the Californian of Mexican descent was box-office gold in his home state. He drew hordes of fans to the iconic Olympic Auditorium in Los Angeles and Legion Stadium in Hollywood.

In total, Ortiz fought nineteen times at the Olympic and thirty-three times at Legion Stadium, making him a true hometown hero and ticket seller. When he was on the bill, anything going on in other states and weight classes didn't matter.

Ortiz eventually blossomed into a well-rounded fighter who could use any style necessary to get the win, but he had to overcome some growing pains that saw him start off with a so-so 17–9 record. He certainly found his groove, winning twenty-one of his next twenty-five bouts to earn a shot at the bantamweight title held by a man who had previously beaten him, Lou Salica.

The second time around, it was all Ortiz, and he took a unanimous decision and the championship. Ortiz reigned for nearly five years, successfully defending his crown fifteen times, beating Salica again and finally avenging his losses to Goldberg.

As champion, Ortiz won thirty-five of thirty-seven bouts (nontitle fights included, with the only blemishes a loss to fellow hall-of-famer Willie Pep and a draw with Carlos Chávez). In January 1947, he lost his title to Harold Dade but then regained it two months later before defending it another four times.

Vic Toweel took the title for good in 1950 in South Africa, but Ortiz had nothing to hang his head about. He had already made his mark on the sport as a 118-pound legend both at home and abroad.

MANNY PACQUIAO

 **"PAC-MAN"**

GENERAL SANTOS CITY, PHILIPPINES
BORN: December 17, 1978
HEIGHT: 5'5½"
RECORD: 62–8–2 (39 KOs)
TITLES WON: World Champion at Flyweight, Junior Featherweight, Featherweight, Junior Lightweight, Lightweight, Junior Welterweight, Welterweight, and Junior Middleweight
HALL OF FAME INDUCTION: 2025

Someday they're going to make a movie about the life of Manny Pacquiao. And no one's going to believe it.

That's how incredible the journey of "Pac-Man" has been. From street kid in Manila, to a world titleholder in a record eight weight classes, to pro basketball player and senator, Pacquiao's story is one for the ages. He's also a hero to the entire nation of the Philippines, as well as an icon around the world.

"The man signed seventy-five autographs at least, [with] people waiting in line for an hour after his run," said Sean Gibbons, president of Pacquiao's MP Promotions, of a typical day of training. "He's contagious. He tells you always, 'Just stay humble, believe in God,' and just being around him—I'll never be able to achieve this level of boxing again around someone like this. It doesn't happen in many lifetimes, and there's no one that pulls people like he does again from all parts of the world."

With his ever-present smile and an infectious attitude, it's easy to see why casual observers flocked to see Pacquiao. And when it comes to boxing, Pacquiao's speed, power, and two-fisted attack allowed him to move up from 112 to 154 pounds and excel every step of the way.

His resume reads like a who's who of boxing, with wins over Juan Manuel Márquez, Marco Antonio Barrera, Erik Morales, Oscar De La Hoya, Ricky Hatton, Miguel Cotto, Shane Mosley, and Timothy Bradley. Those are all hall-of-famers, and Pacquiao beat them all.

A SuperFight with Floyd Mayweather Jr. in 2015 happened several years too late, with Mayweather taking a twelve-round unanimous decision victory. Still, that blemish didn't affect Pacquiao's legacy in the slightest: he was a shoo-in for Canastota's class of 2025, his first year of eligibility.

WILLIE PEP

★★★★★ "WILL O' THE WISP" ★★★★★

HARTFORD, CT
BORN: September 19, 1922
DIED: November 23, 2006
HEIGHT: 5'5"
RECORD: 229–11–1 (65 KOs)
TITLES WON: World Featherweight Champion
HALL OF FAME INDUCTION: 1990

Pernell Whitaker, the greatest defensive boxer of the modern era, didn't hand out praise lightly. But when I asked him about the man many consider to be the greatest defensive boxer of all time, "Sweet Pea" had to give it up for Willie Pep.

"Of course," said Whitaker of Pep's prowess in the art of "hit and don't get hit." "I've seen his videos, and I agree with that. Back in his time, that was his era. I watched quite a few of his fights on tape... Willie Pep was one of the greats."

Coming from us, that's one thing. Coming from a fellow boxer is a whole other level of respect. Pep, the longtime featherweight champion who retired from the sport with a remarkable record of 229–11–1 with sixty-five knockouts, may have been your favorite fighter's favorite fighter.

Make no mistake about it: Pep's boxing skills were sublime, and in his chest beat the heart of a fighter.

Just look at his four-fight series with Sandy Saddler, a series of brutal, foul-filled wars that forced both men to go into some dark places in search of victory.

Saddler won three of the four bouts, but the end results don't determine Pep's place in boxing history; they just add a chapter to a bigger story that saw Connecticut's "Will o' the Wisp" leave an indelible mark on a sport that saw him go into practically every fight knowing that he likely couldn't hurt his opponent. That takes guts, along with the speed, footwork, and fight IQ that became his hallmark.

And although the legendary recount of him winning a round against Jackie Graves without throwing a single punch is disputed, what's not up for debate is the fighter's legendary resilience.

In January 1947, Pep was involved in a plane crash.

Three people died, and Pep was one of eleven survivors; he suffered a fractured back and leg in the accident.

Against all odds, he recovered from his injuries and fought on, firing off twenty-six wins in a row to improve his remarkable record to 134–1–1. Pep didn't lose a second fight until he faced Saddler the first time in October 1948, just twenty-one months after he almost lost his life.

Now that's a fighter.

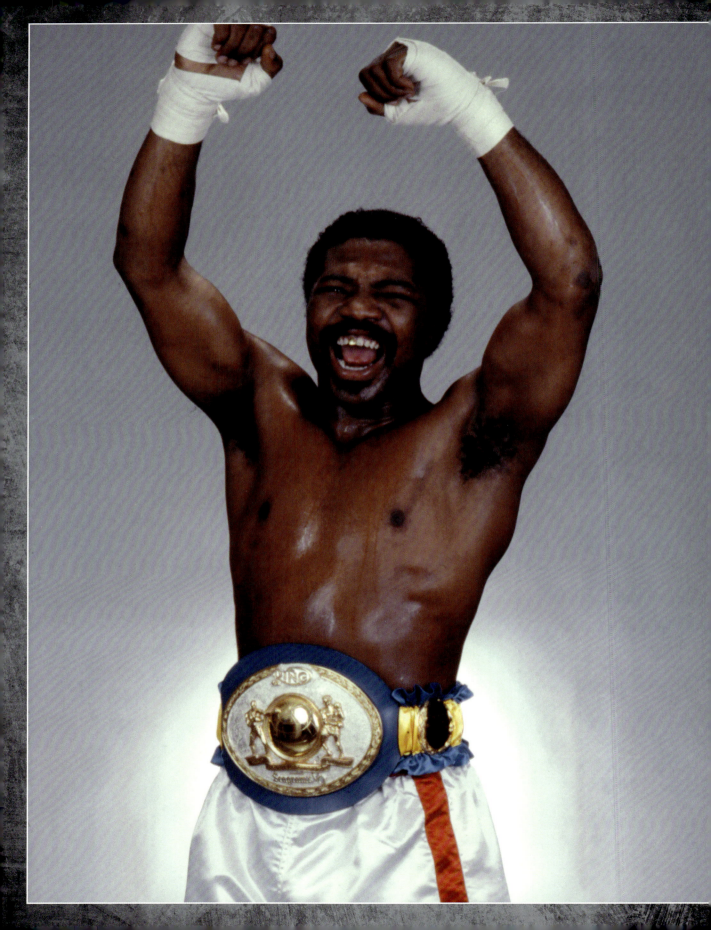

AARON PRYOR

 "THE HAWK"

CINCINNATI, OH
BORN: October 20, 1955
DIED: October 9, 2016
HEIGHT: 5'6"
RECORD: 39–1 (35 KOs)
TITLES WON: World Junior Welterweight Champion
HALL OF FAME INDUCTION: 1996

Throwing punches from all angles while aggressively chasing down his opponents, Cincinnati's Aaron Pryor had little regard for his own safety in the ring. The world adored him for it.

A top-flight amateur who compiled more than two hundred wins, Pryor boasted a fighting style that was actually better suited for the pros. He ran through his first twenty-four fights without a loss, and fight 25 saw him rise from a first-round knockdown to take the junior welterweight title from Antonio Cervantes in the second stanza.

Title defenses against Dujuan Johnson and Akio Kameda also saw the reckless Pryor hit the deck, but as usual, he came back to knock out his foes. All that was left for the 31–0 Pryor was a SuperFight, and he got one on November 12, 1982, against Alexis Argüello. It was anticipated to be an action fight, but the boxers took it to another level in one of the best fights of all time.

"I hit the guy with everything I had, and he was laughing at me," said Argüello. "Let me tell you one thing: The guy was a fast guy, he was so quick, and what scared me the most was that, in the fourteenth round, I was tired, so I thought that he would be tired, too. But the guy came on like a storm. It was a great battle. The first one in Miami? What a fight. Those fourteen rounds. Every time I see them, I start to sweat. The guy was good. And he was there with heart and soul and with a purpose."

Pryor's fourteenth-round TKO of Argüello was followed by a tenth-round knockout in their 1983 rematch. Unfortunately, drugs took over his life and did what his opponents couldn't: They stopped "The Hawk."

A 1987 comeback resulted in a defeat to Bobby Joe Young. Pryor ended his career with three wins, but the glory days were over until he received his place in the hall of fame in 1996.

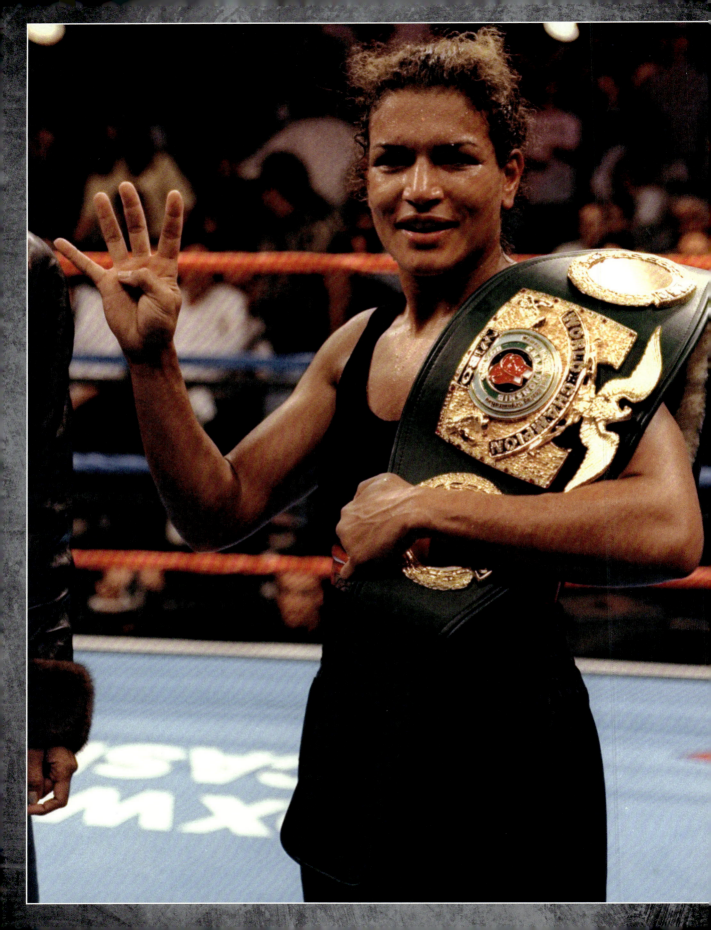

LUCIA RIJKER

"THE DUTCH DESTROYER"

AMSTERDAM, NETHERLANDS
BORN: December 6, 1967
HEIGHT: 5'6"
RECORD: 17–0 (14 KOs)
TITLES WON: None
HALL OF FAME INDUCTION: 2020

If you cover combat sports for a living, being intimidated by some of the toughest athletes in the world can't be part of the gig.

But Lucia Rijker scared me. She just had an intensity that put me on guard from the moment we got on the phone together. In 2019, a couple decades after that first interview, "The Dutch Destroyer" was part of the first class of women inducted into the International Boxing Hall of Fame. I reminded her of that intensity. She laughed.

"Yeah, I was crazy," Rijker said. "I had such pride. That's why I went after Christy Martin. She insulted me. There was no one on this planet that could insult me without being confronted by me. That's how I thought. I didn't care how big you were . . . I was committed. If I said it, I was gonna be in your face about it. I was fearless."

That attitude carried into the ring, where Rijker followed up an unbeaten kickboxing career with an equally perfect career in the sweet science, establishing herself as the best in the business from 1996 to 2004. Simply put, Rijker's technique—both offensively and defensively—was flawless. She had power and a chin, and when you add in that trademark intensity, her only issue was finding people to fight her.

Christy Martin, female boxing's biggest star, was willing to do it, and a bout was set for July 30, 2005. "The Coal Miner's Daughter" matched Rijker in intensity, and some bad blood quickly got boiling. The situation was so tense that Rijker even showed up at Martin's prefight workout for the media at the LA Boxing Club. Someone asked when her next fight was. Rijker responded, "In a few seconds."

There was an altercation between the two but, unfortunately, no official fight—Rijker ruptured her Achilles tendon, canceling the bout, which had guaranteed the winner a then-record million-dollar purse. The two superstars never met in the ring; they saw each other only at hall of fame events to celebrate their greatness. And that's okay with Rijker.

"Who would have known that that kid, when she was seven [and decided to be a fighter], would be at the place today where she's at in the hall of fame," Rijker said. "That, to me, is almost like a miracle. It's almost like my life was a movie."

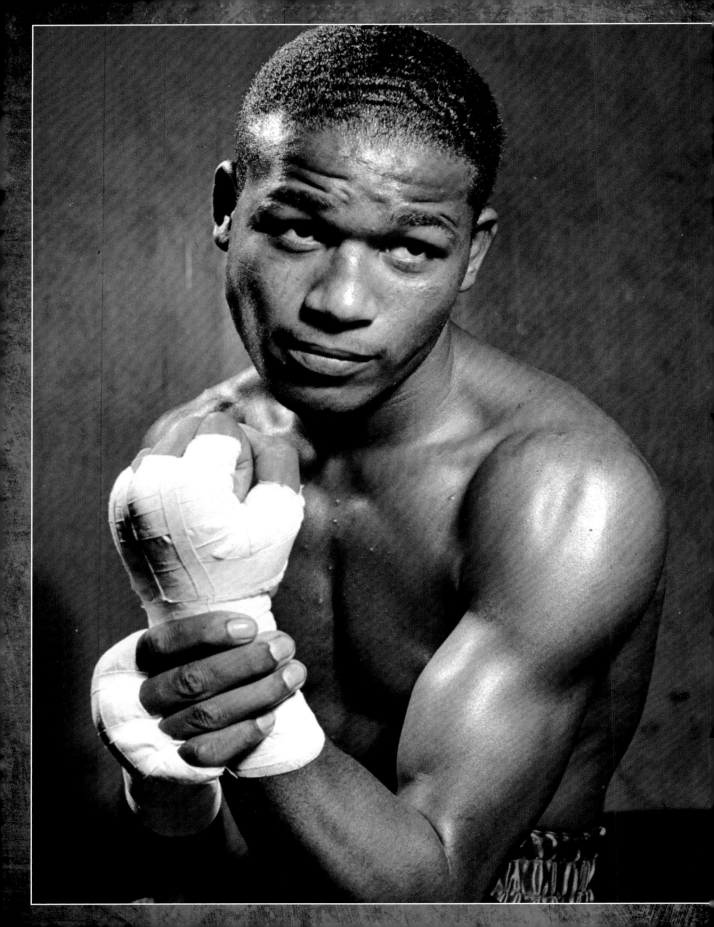

SUGAR RAY ROBINSON

NEW YORK, NY
BORN: May 3, 1921
DIED: April 12, 1989
HEIGHT: 5'11"
RECORD: 174–19–6, 2 NC (109 KOs)
TITLES WON: World Welterweight and Middleweight Champion
HALL OF FAME INDUCTION: 1990

Pound for pound. It was a phrase coined for Sugar Ray Robinson to let the world know who the best boxer in the world was, regardless of weight class.

Robinson was indeed that guy—not just during his active career, but of all time.

Robinson was the prototype of what an elite boxer should be. In addition to having all the physical tools (size, speed, and reflexes), Robinson boasted flawless technique, a rock-solid chin, and heart for days. He was also able to knock out opponents or outbox them for fifteen rounds. Throw in genius fight IQ, and the man born Walker Smith Jr. was the perfect fighting machine.

Having all those attributes on paper is wonderful, but to truly be great, Robinson had to show it all in the ring. And like Michael Jordan in basketball or Tom Brady in football, when the spotlight was at its brightest, Robinson was at his best.

A five-time middleweight champion, Robinson was considered by most observers to have been at his peak when he was a welterweight. He won the title at 147 pounds in 1946 by defeating Tommy Bell. He also defeated Fritzie Zivic, Kid Gavilán, Jake LaMotta, and Henry Armstrong during his time in the division, and he lost only once to LaMotta—a defeat he avenged five times. Unfortunately, precious little footage of Robinson's time at welterweight exists, but his greatness was still fully on display when he moved to the 160-pound weight class.

There, he continued with what ultimately topped out as a ninety-one-fight winning streak and won the middleweight title by stopping LaMotta in their sixth meeting in 1951, dubbed "The St. Valentine's Day Massacre." Five months later, Robinson's streak came to a shocking end when he lost his title to underdog Randy Turpin, but he took his belt back just two months later via a tenth-round TKO.

With the stars aligned again, Robinson got back to work. He engaged in memorable series with Carmen Basilio and Gene Fullmer that showcased his grit, grace, and greatness as he traded the 160-pound belt back and forth with the popular sluggers.

Inevitably, though, Father Time caught up. Robinson called it quits in 1965, with nothing left to be said about a legendary run that will likely never be touched.

Sweet as sugar, they said about him. And he was, pound for pound.

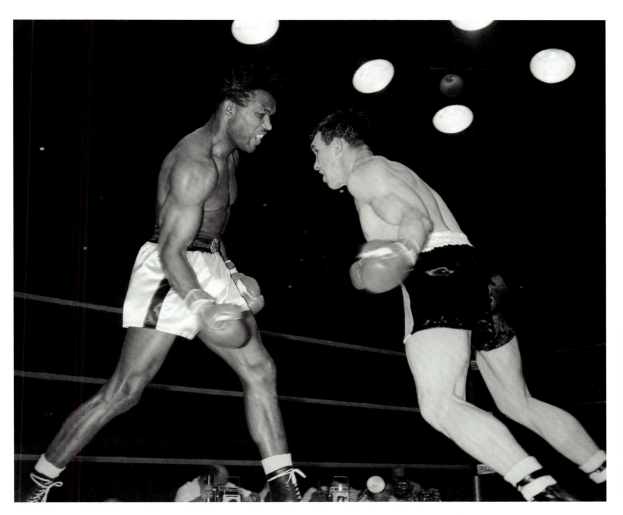

BARNEY ROSS

NEW YORK, NY
BORN: December 23, 1909
DIED: January 18, 1967
HEIGHT: 5'7"
RECORD: 72–4–3 (22 KOs)
TITLES WON: World Champion at Lightweight,
Junior Welterweight, and Welterweight
HALL OF FAME INDUCTION: 1990

The fighting wasn't over for Barney Ross when he retired from the sport of boxing in 1938. Instead, it was just beginning for the proud Jewish warrior, who joined the United States Marine Corps and fought for his country in World War II.

Ross, always a courageous battler in the ring, carried that over to his time overseas. He fought in the Battle of Guadalcanal and received the Silver Star for valor in combat. It was the perfect example of life imitating art. However, it has to be noted that Ross's artistry in the ring was also as real as it gets.

Only the third boxer to win titles in three different weight classes, Ross was a tireless worker in the ring, with the ability to box or bang with equal effectiveness. As for his chin, it was made of granite: In seventy-nine bouts, he was never knocked out. That alone is an amazing feat, considering that he shared the ring with fellow greats Henry Armstrong, Jimmy McLarnin, and Tony Canzoneri.

It was Canzoneri who Ross defeated in 1933 for the lightweight and junior welterweight titles. In May 1934, Ross added the welterweight crown to his trophy case by beating McLarnin. Four months later, he lost the title back to McLarnin, but he then rallied to win his next twenty-one fights. In the process, he took the title once more from McLarnin in the finale of a trilogy that displayed all the best aspects of the sport at its highest level. That cemented Ross's place as one of the best—not only of his era, but of all time.

TOMMY RYAN

REDWOOD, NY
BORN: March 31, 1870
DIED: August 3, 1948
HEIGHT: 5'7½"
RECORD: 87–2–14, 3 NC (68 KOs)
TITLES WON: World Champion at Middleweight and Welterweight
HALL OF FAME INDUCTION: 1991

In the late 1800s and early 1900s, boxing was more of a street fight than anything else. Tommy Ryan changed that, largely introducing science into the sweet science. He studied every aspect of the game, introduced the idea of fighting out of a crouch—which he later taught to heavyweight champion James J. Jeffries—and could baffle any opponent with his technique and smarts.

In the wild, wild west that was professional boxing in those days, win-loss records and match dates are often sketchy. The general consensus is that Ryan fought anywhere from 99 to 106 fights, winning or drawing in all but a handful of them. He won world titles in both the welterweight and middleweight divisions, where he is considered among the best of all time.

Ryan was an iron man as well, participating in bouts that went seventy-six and fifty-seven rounds against Danny Needham and Jimmy Murphy, respectively. He also scored victories over "Mysterious" Billy Smith and "Nonpareil" Jack Dempsey. In an amazing factoid, Ryan never lost his welterweight or middleweight titles in the ring; instead, he relinquished his welterweight crown to chase after the top prize at middleweight. After taking that title from Bill Heffernan in his second try in 1897, Ryan successfully defended it twelve times before he retired in 1907.

MATTHEW SAAD MUHAMMAD

 "MIRACLE MATTHEW"

PHILADELPHIA, PA
BORN: June 16, 1954
DIED: May 25, 2014
HEIGHT: 5'11"
RECORD: 39–16–3 (29 KOs)
TITLES WON: World Light Heavyweight Champion
HALL OF FAME INDUCTION: 1998

Every man or woman who walks up those four steps into a boxing ring has heart. But some have a little extra. Fans loved Matthew Saad Muhammad because he had a lot extra.

It proved that greatness comes in all forms. Even if "Miracle Matthew" hadn't been an elite action fighter with otherworldly resilience, odds are good that people would have still gravitated to him simply because of his backstory.

Born Maxwell Antonio Loach, he was renamed Matthew Franklin by the nuns who took him in as a five-year-old when he was abandoned by the family entrusted to take care of him after his mother died.

This harrowing beginning made what he ultimately faced in the boxing ring pale in comparison. When he did get in trouble in the ring, he fought back with a fury, knowing that what he saw outside the ropes was worse than just having to face one man in battle.

And battle he did. Saad Muhammad won the WBC light heavyweight title in 1979 with an eighth-round TKO of Marvin Johnson. He went on to hold that belt until he lost to Dwight Muhammad Qawi in 1981.

In between those fights, Saad Muhammad (who changed his name after converting to Islam) produced an epic title reign that included eight successful defenses, victories over top contenders in the light heavyweight division's Golden Age, and an undeniable classic with Yaqui López in 1980 that saw him take twenty unanswered blows before he stormed back to stop the challenger in the fourteenth round.

Saad Muhammad continued to fight for another eleven years after he lost his title. Sadly, he died in 2014 at the age of fifty-nine.

SANDY SADDLER

BOSTON, MA
BORN: June 23, 1926
DIED: September 18, 2001
HEIGHT: 5'8½"
RECORD: 145–16–2 (104 KOs)
TITLES WON: World Featherweight Champion
HALL OF FAME INDUCTION: 1990

The first thing that comes to mind when talking about Sandy Saddler is his four-bout series with fellow hall-of-famer Willie Pep. But those were just four of his 163 professional fights, a slate made even more impressive by the fact that he had to retire in 1956 at just 30 years old due to a detached retina suffered in a car accident.

At the time, Saddler was still the featherweight champion of the world, a title he held for six years during his second reign atop the decision. The first began in 1948, when he stunningly stopped Pep in four rounds, ending the Connecticut native's 73-fight winning streak in emphatic fashion. Pep regained the crown four months later, but it was Saddler winning their next two bouts, fights that were highlighted (or lowlighted) by fouls and brutal infighting.

That "take no prisoners" attack epitomized Saddler's style, one heavyweight great George Foreman vividly described after the New England native's death in 2001.

"As a boxer, Sandy was vicious," Foreman told ESPN. "There is no other word to describe him in the ring. When he was in the ring, he knew nothing about retreat. Everything was about get him, get him, get him."

More often than not, Saddler got his man. Owner of a 72 percent knockout rate, the lanky puncher finished more opponents than any other featherweight champion, and those 104 knockouts are sixth on the all-time KO list. And with wins over the likes of Joe Brown, Lauro Salas, and Flash Elorde, plus a second reign that was expected to last even longer than the six years it already had before fate intervened, Saddler's place among the greats is secure.

SALVADOR SÁNCHEZ

★★★★★ "CHAVA" ★★★★★

TIANGUISTENCO, MEXICO
BORN: January 26, 1959
DIED: August 12, 1982
HEIGHT: 5'6"
RECORD: 44–1–1 (32 KOs)
TITLES WON: World Featherweight Champion
HALL OF FAME INDUCTION: 1991

Boxing has always been a game of "what ifs." What if this fight happened? What if the referee didn't stop a bout when he did? What if the judges got it right?

But perhaps the greatest "what if" in the sport surrounded Salvador Sánchez. What if the Mexican featherweight didn't die in a tragic automobile accident in 1982?

Consider that he made this list despite perhaps never having reached his physical prime.

A defensive wizard with laserlike accuracy and thudding power, the Tianguistenco native brought a stellar 33-1-1 record into his first title shot against veteran champion Danny "Little Red" Lopez, but there was more than a little skepticism about the soft-spoken challenger.

"He might as well have been fighting unemployed shepherds and vacationing streetcar conductors when you look at the line of guys he fought," the *Newark Star-Ledger*'s Jerry Izenberg said of Sánchez's level of opposition.

But good is good, and when he faced Lopez on February 2, 1980, he showed the world what he had in his head, chest, and fists. Sánchez nearly shut out the champion before the fight was stopped in the thirteenth round.

Sánchez was a champion at the tender age of twenty-one. Although there were still some skeptics, over the next two-and-a-half years, he silenced them all in what could easily be described as a golden age for the 126-pound weight class.

Within four months of his title-winning effort in Phoenix, he defeated one of the best fighters to never win a championship, Ruben Castillo, and halted Lopez in their rematch. Two more successful defenses over Pat Ford and Juan La Porte capped off a spectacular 1980 campaign. In 1981, "Chava" logged four more wins, the biggest of which was in an August SuperFight against Puerto Rican star Wilfredo Gómez.

Coming into the fight at Caesars Palace in Las Vegas, Gómez was unbeaten in thirty-three fights, with all thirty-two of his victories coming by way of knockout. His move to the featherweight division after a reign of terror at 122 pounds was seen as the next step in his coronation as his island's greatest boxer.

But the fight was all Sánchez as the Mexican battered Gómez and dropped him twice en route to an eighth-round TKO victory. If the world didn't already know who Salvador Sánchez was, it did now.

Fans got to enjoy the ring wizardry of the featherweight king only three more times. His life ended on a highway 145 miles north of Mexico when his Porsche slammed into a cargo truck and pickup, killing him instantly. It was just three weeks after Sánchez, a married father of two sons, had defeated Azumah Nelson in Madison Square Garden on July 21, 1982, at the age of twenty-three.

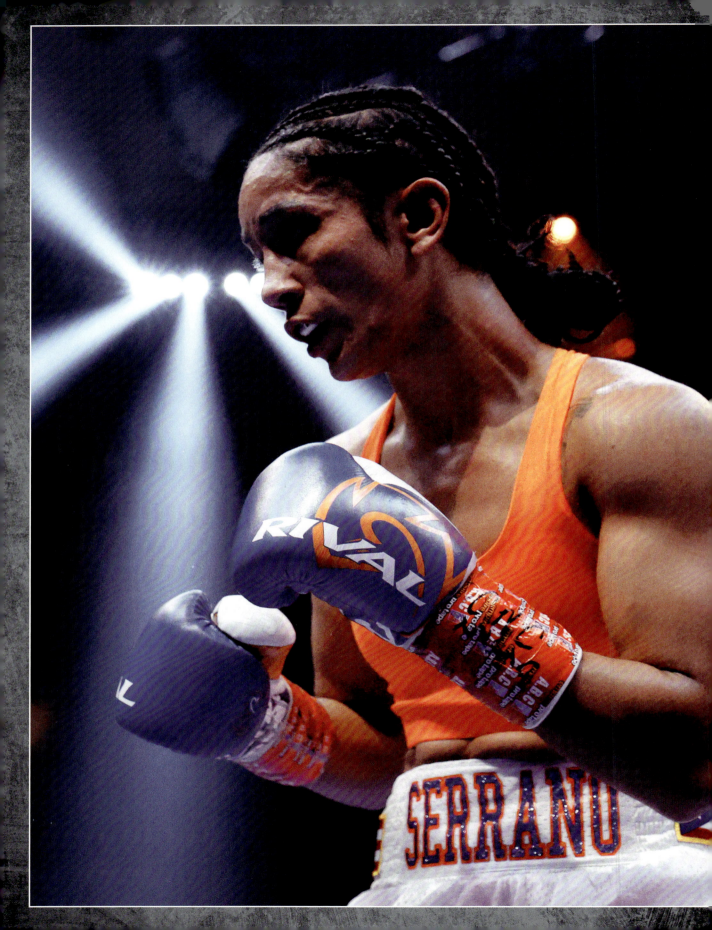

AMANDA SERRANO

 "THE REAL DEAL"

CAROLINA, PUERTO RICO
BORN: October 9, 1988
HEIGHT: 5′5½″
RECORD: 47–3–1 (31 KOs)*
TITLES WON: World Champion at Featherweight,
Junior Bantamweight, Junior Welterweight, Bantamweight,
Junior Lightweight, Junior Featherweight, and Lightweight

*As of press date

Amanda Serrano never pictured becoming one of the greatest female boxers of all time. She just wanted to hang out at the gym with her big sister, Cindy.

"At first, it was all fun and games," Serrano said. "I wasn't in the sport to become a world champion. I just did it for the fun."

Well, winning was fun, and once the native of Carolina, Puerto Rico, laced up the gloves and started getting her hand raised, it became an addiction. So much so that "The Real Deal" has now won world titles in seven weight classes, a feat recognized by the Guinness Book of World Records in 2019.

Part of this was her talent, another was her punching power, and yet another was her work ethic. But perhaps the biggest key to Serrano's success has been her dedication to the sport. Through all the good, bad, and ugly of the fight game, Serrano's focus never wavered. A big—and soon to become tiresome—storyline on her way to superstardom was that she didn't even have a cellphone.

"I think they're fascinated with the no cellphone," Serrano said. "Nowadays, everybody's stuck on their phones, everybody's looking down, they're never looking up, and it's a headache. It's a hassle having to answer back to so many people. And there are no distractions. I have my family that keeps me on my Ps and Qs. That makes me happy, and that's all I need."

That focus took her to the top of the boxing world in 2022, when she and Katie Taylor combined to not only sell out Madison Square Garden and deliver perhaps the greatest fight in women's boxing history, but to each garner a record one-million-dollar purse. It's rare to call one fight a game changer, but for women's boxing, Taylor v. Serrano I did just that.

But Serrano is not finished yet. And even after a highly controversial decision loss to Taylor in a 2024 rematch viewed by millions on Netflix, she is determined to continue raising the bar for the sport she fell into by accident.

CLARESSA SHIELDS

★★★★★ "T-REX" ★★★★★

FLINT, MI
BORN: March 17, 1995
HEIGHT: 5'8"
RECORD: 16–0 (3 KOs)*
TITLES WON: World Champion at Junior Middleweight, Middleweight, Light Heavyweight, Heavyweight, and Super Middleweight

*As of press date

Claressa Shields was right all along. The Flint, Michigan, native told us for years that she was the GWOAT, which stands for Greatest Woman of All Time, but we didn't believe her.

How could this kid make such a claim without hitting the age of thirty and with less than a decade as a professional under her belt?

Well, before turning the big three-o, Shields won two Olympic gold medals for the United States (something no US boxer, male or female, has achieved), turned pro, and then went on to win world titles in five weight classes from 154 pounds to heavyweight.

GWOAT? Absolutely. But if the rest of the boxing world doesn't agree, that's not going to stop her.

"If was a man, I'd be the face of boxing," said Shields. "I've got more accomplishments than everybody. I'm just gonna keep continuing to build myself and let the world accept me and women's boxing."

Shields has already broken new ground, joining with fellow Olympian Katie Taylor to bring women's boxing to audiences never exposed to the sport previously. And though some say that Shields's level of competition doesn't match her talent, a boxer can only fight who's available, and a look at her perfect record shows that "T-Rex" has taken on—and beaten—an impressive list of foes, including Savannah Marshall, Christina Hammer, Marie-Ève Dicaire, Maricela Cornejo, Hanna Rankin, Hannah Gabriels, and Franchón Crews-Dezurn. She plans on continuing to face all comers, because that's just how you become the GWOAT.

"I'm not afraid to take those tough fights," Shields said. "You put somebody in there with me who's good, I'm gonna show you I'm great. Put me in there with somebody who you think is great, I'm gonna show you that I'm phenomenal."

MICHAEL SPINKS

ST. LOUIS, MO
BORN: July 22, 1956
HEIGHT: 6'2½"
RECORD: 31–1 (21 KOs)
TITLES WON: World Light Heavyweight and Heavyweight Champion; 1976 Olympic Gold Medalist
HALL OF FAME INDUCTION: 1994

Michael Spinks and his older brother Leon made history in 1976 as brothers who won Olympic gold medals in the Montreal games. But when Leon turned pro and defeated the legendary Muhammad Ali in just his eighth pro fight for the world heavyweight title in 1978, all eyes moved away from Michael.

That was okay with the soft-spoken younger brother, who got to ply his trade outside the media spotlight that engulfed his sibling. As Leon grappled with the trappings of fame, Michael became one of the greatest light heavyweights not just of his era, but of all time.

Strangely, it almost wasn't to be. Spinks didn't expect to turn professional after he won his gold medal. He returned to work at a chemical factory in his native St. Louis, but with his mother to take care of, he decided to enter the punch-for-pay ranks. He debuted in April 1977 with a first-round TKO of Eddie Benson. By the time Leon upset Ali, Michael was 7–0 and moving fast.

The Spinks train, now driven by Michael after Leon lost to Ali in their rematch, picked up speed in the ensuing years, thanks to a right hand known as "The Spinks Jinx" and a willingness to fight all comers in what might have been the best collection of light heavyweight talent ever seen.

From Murray Sutherland and Yaqui López to Marvin Johnson and Eddie Mustafa Muhammad, Spinks beat them all. When he defeated Dwight Muhammad Qawi for the undisputed light heavyweight crown in 1983, Spinks had done it all at 175 pounds.

So what next? He moved to heavyweight, where he upset longtime champion Larry Holmes

to win the IBF world championship in 1985. After defeating Holmes a second time and knocking out Steffen Tangstad and Gerry Cooney, Spinks suffered the lone loss of his career to a prime Mike Tyson in June 1988.

Spinks never fought again, content with a body of work that landed him in the International Boxing Hall of Fame in 1994.

YOUNG STRIBLING

MACON, GA
BORN: December 26, 1904
DIED: October 3, 1933
HEIGHT: 6'1"
RECORD: 224–13–14, 2 NC (129 KOs)
TITLES WON: None
HALL OF FAME INDUCTION: 1996

Another classic example of what might have been, William Lawrence "Young" Stribling Jr. put together a hall-of-fame career in the 1920s and early 1930s despite perhaps not even reaching his fighting prime. His life was cut short in a motorcycle accident when he was only 28 years old.

Despite this tragic end, Stribling's career was a rousing success. The skinny bantamweight teenager ended up fighting heavyweights (including Primo Carnera twice) and light heavyweights as he literally grew up in the fight game.

The Georgia native made 253 appearances in the ring and left 224 times with his hand raised in victory, with 129 of those wins coming by knockout. Included on his resume were wins over some of the best of his era, including Jimmy Slattery, Battling Levinsky, and Jimmy Delaney.

Stribling nearly won a world title three times. Once was against Mike McTigue at light heavyweight, where he was given a referee's decision before the referee later overturned that verdict to a controversial draw.

After a 1926 loss to Paul Berlenbach in his second crack at a title, he moved up a division. In 1931, he gave heavyweight champion Max Schmeling a tough battle but was stopped in the fifteenth and final round.

Undeterred, Stribling got right back to work, going 18–2 with one NC in his final twenty-one bouts. Unfortunately, his untimely death put a halt on any dreams of a world championship.

Largely lost to history, despite the efforts of fight historians to put his name back in the public consciousness, Stribling eventually was recognized by the boxing community with his induction into the International Boxing Hall of Fame in 1996.

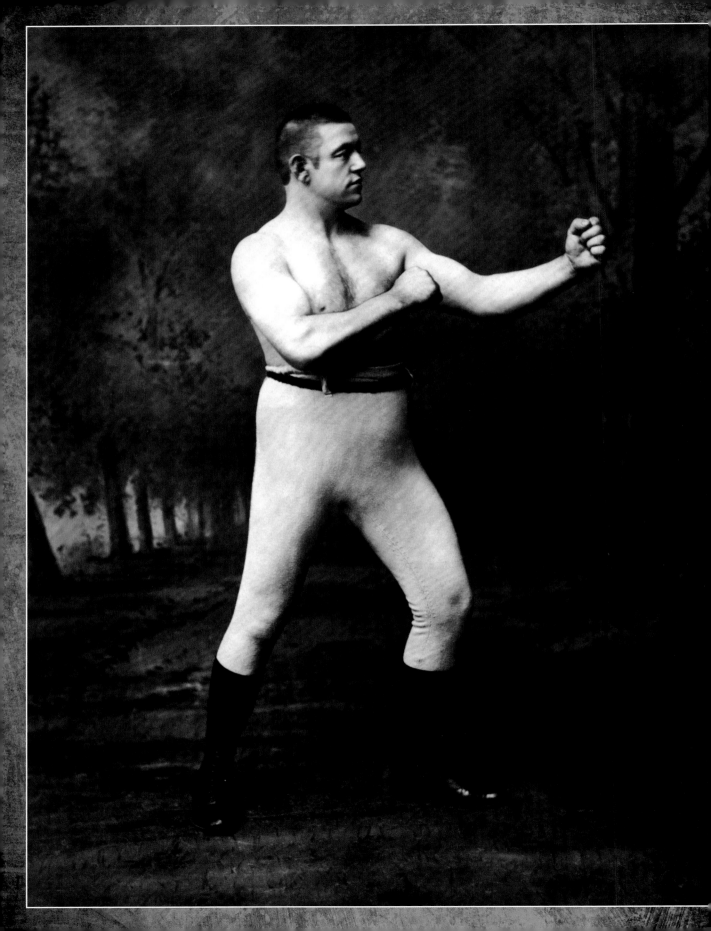

JOHN L. SULLIVAN

 "THE BOSTON STRONG BOY"

ROXBURY, MA
BORN: October 15, 1858
DIED: February 2, 1918
HEIGHT: 5'10½"
RECORD: 38–1–1 (32 KOs)
TITLES WON: World Heavyweight Champion
HALL OF FAME INDUCTION: 1990

John L. Sullivan was "the baddest man on the planet."

He wasn't shy about letting everyone know it, either. As the last of the bare-knuckle champions and the first gloved heavyweight champion, he was famous for walking into bars and declaring, "I can lick any sonofabitch in the house."

Those are some pretty tough words. Clint Eastwood famously said in the boxing film *Million Dollar Baby* that "tough ain't enough," but back in the late 1800s, it was. And few walked the walk better than Sullivan, who backed up his boasts with his fists. He took on and beat all comers as he traveled around the United States, competing in what was then an outlaw sport, with rules barely resembling those that govern professional boxing today.

Nonetheless, Sullivan is widely held to be America's first sports superstar. His exploits were splashed on the pages of newspapers, he was reported to be the highest-paid athlete of his time, and his bouts were attended by the likes of the James brothers (Jesse and Frank) and Oscar Wilde.

Despite an impressive collection of iconic fights, no Sullivan bout captured the imagination of the world like his July 8, 1889, meeting with Jake Kilrain. A fight like no other, this one went seventy-five rounds—yes, seventy-five rounds. Note that rounds ended when one of the combatants was knocked down or thrown down, meaning that a single stanza could be seconds or hours long. After two hours, sixteen minutes, and twenty-five seconds, Kilrain's corner threw in the towel. Sullivan was still the baddest man on the planet, even if he and Kilrain were both later arrested for participating in the illegal bout.

On September 7, 1892, Sullivan finally met his match in the slick-boxing Jim Corbett, who knocked out "The Boston Strong Boy" in the twenty-first round under the Marquess of Queensberry rules. It proved that, as any sport evolves, some are left behind. But although modern boxing wasn't going to wait for John L. Sullivan, he undoubtedly left a mark never to be forgotten.

JOHNNY TAPIA

 **"MI VIDA LOCA"**

ALBUQUERQUE, NM
BORN: February 13, 1967
DIED: May 27, 2012
HEIGHT: 5'6"
RECORD: 59–5–2 (30 KOs)
TITLES WON: World Champion at Super Flyweight, Bantamweight, and Featherweight
HALL OF FAME INDUCTION: 2017

Back in the stone age, when I was trying to find a place in the boxing world, I designed Johnny Tapia's first website. It wasn't very good, but hey, it was the late 1990s. Long story short, in those early days of the Internet, it still would have been easy to receive emails from fans and answer them that way.

Not for Johnny Tapia. Instead, he insisted that I fax over all the emails. He then answered them while we were on the phone. And this wasn't typical fan mail: Tapia received harrowing stories from people who found a kindred spirit in a man haunted by past and present demons, including the murder of his mother and various bouts with substance abuse.

As every phone call ended, he simply said, "Pray for me."

"Anything I do, I'm a professional at it—alcoholic, doper, addict, whatever you want to call it," Tapia said. "But for some reason, I'm still here. I've basically done everything I could do."

When he died in 2012 from heart failure (far too young, at the age of forty-five), it shook the boxing world to its core. Although his accomplishments in the ring were impressive—he won fifty-nine fights, including seventeen world title fights across three weight classes—his impact outside the ring was even greater. The popular pride of Albuquerque, New Mexico, Tapia openly lived his troubled life in the public eye and showed others who were struggling that there was a way out.

The words tattooed on his stomach, "Mi Vida Loca" (My Crazy Life), spoke volumes, but his wife, Teresa, said it best when it came to her husband's appeal.

"I believe it's because they feel that they're on the same level with him," she said. "There are so many people who are great fighters in the world, but the average fan looks at them as great fighters and they feel that they're untouchable. [With] Johnny, because of the problems he's had in his life and the tragedies that he's endured and survived, they feel on the same level as him and they can relate to him. It may be a grandfather talking about his son or a mother talking about her loss, and Johnny has so many areas in his life where he can help people, whether it's drugs, pain, losing a loved one, losing someone that was murdered, abandonment—there's so many issues that he can cover, so that's why people can relate."

KATIE TAYLOR

★★★★★

BRAY, IRELAND
BORN: July 2, 1986
HEIGHT: 5'5"
RECORD: 24–1 (6 KOs)*
TITLES WON: World Champion at Lightweight and Junior Welterweight

*As of press date

A global star and an icon in her native Ireland, Katie Taylor couldn't have found anywhere farther from the bright lights than Connecticut, where she has lived and trained for most of her professional boxing career.

That's the way the soft-spoken Taylor likes it, and when I made my way to the Manchester Ring of Champions Society gym to visit the 2012 Olympic gold medalist, I pointed out that there was no designated parking spot for her and no banner proclaiming that this was her training home, two items that several of her gym mates had.

She smiled and let me know that she didn't need a banner or a parking spot, confirming her as an athlete who was content to let her fists do the talking.

"I don't really buy into the hype about myself, or anybody else," said Taylor. "I think I have a fantastic team of people around me, I have a fantastic family around me, and if I ever was getting a bit too big for my boots, those are people that will actually step in line to help me."

Taylor—despite being someone who won't flood social media with her every move, get into trash-talking wars with opponents, or look for the spotlight—brought women's boxing to new heights when she won gold in London in 2012, the first year the sport was featured in the Olympics.

She was just getting started, though. A shot at a second Olympic medal came up short in 2016, but a few months later she convinced boxing promoter Eddie Hearn that women's boxing could be a moneymaker. Hearn took a chance and Taylor proved to be correct.

Headlining shows, filling arenas and winning championships on cards televised worldwide, Taylor was a juggernaut. She won a lightweight world title in her seventh pro fight against Anahí Ester Sánchez and never looked back, becoming a unified champion at 135 and 140 pounds.

The biggest impact was on April 30, 2022, when Taylor and Amanda Serrano headlined Madison Square Garden in a bout that earned each fighter a one-million-dollar purse, a first for women's boxing. It was well worth the hype, as the pair delivered perhaps the greatest fight in women's boxing history, with Taylor taking a close decision that further cemented her place as one of the best to ever do it.

"I think we both elevated the sport and lifted it to a new level," said Taylor, who repeated her win over Serrano in their 2024 rematch. "Over the years, both of us have broken down so many barriers to get to this point, and this fight will have inspired so many young girls. That's the most satisfying thing for me about this whole journey. Everyone talks about Ali and Frazier when it comes to boxing at Madison Square Garden and now our fight will be included in those conversations as well for decades to come."

DICK TIGER

AMAIGBO, NIGERIA
BORN: August 14, 1929
DIED: December 14, 1971
HEIGHT: 5'8"
RECORD: 60–19–3 (27 KOs)
TITLES WON: World Champion at Middleweight and Light Heavyweight
HALL OF FAME INDUCTION: 1991

In an era stacked with tough guys, Dick Tiger may have been the toughest. Only legitimately stopped once in eighty-two fights (an early loss was due to injury), Tiger made the long trips to England and the United States to build a career that made him a hero in his native Nigeria.

A blue-collar battler who won with fundamentals and grit, Tiger was never flashy—but, oh, was he good. After building his resume at home and in England, he made his United States debut at Madison Square Garden in 1959, drawing with Rory Calhoun. A rematch resulted in a controversial decision win for Calhoun, but from then on, Tiger started making his moves.

He split a pair of fights with Joey Giardello; beat top middleweights Holly Mims, "Spider" Webb, Florentino Fernández, and Henry Hank; and, on October 23, 1962, decisioned Gene Fullmer to win the WBA middleweight title. They fought twice more, with Tiger drawing one and winning one. He traded the belt back and forth with Giardello until he lost it for good to Emile Griffith in 1966.

Eight months after dropping the middleweight title, Tiger got right back on the championship horse by beating José Torres for the light heavyweight crown, making two successful title defenses.

Still a force even after losing the belt to fellow great Bob Foster in 1968, Tiger outlasted Frankie DePaula in *The Ring* magazine's Fight of the Year in 1968 and then outpointed Nino Benvenuti in May 1969. But without a rematch with Foster on the horizon, he retired in 1970. Twenty-one years later, one of boxing's great worldwide ambassadors was inducted into the International Boxing Hall of Fame.

JAMES TONEY

 "LIGHTS OUT"

ANN ARBOR, MI
BORN: August 24, 1968
HEIGHT: 5'9"
RECORD: 77–10–3, 2 NC (47 KOs)
TITLES WON: World Champion at Middleweight, Super Middleweight, and Cruiserweight
HALL OF FAME INDUCTION: 2022

True boxing aficionados always appreciated James Toney. A modern-era boxer, active from 1988 to 2017, Toney won three divisional titles and nearly a fourth at heavyweight. Still, you could have easily sent "Lights Out" back in time to the 1940s and '50s, and he would have fit in seamlessly. When I told him as much, the often gruff and standoffish Toney opened up and gladly accepted the compliment.

"Rocky Marciano, Ezzard Charles, Jersey Joe Walcott—those guys were real fighters, and they fought everybody," said Toney. "They were willing to work on their trade, and they were hardcore fighters. Ray Robinson and Archie Moore were the guys I patterned myself after. I don't pattern myself after the new style of fighters. The fighters of yesterday fought when they were injured, with a broken foot or a broken hand. Those were real fighters. That's what I am. I will break somebody down. I can go short and end it early, or I can go late. If I take you deep, you'd better know how to swim. If you don't, you're gonna drown."

Toney talked a lot over the course of his career, but he also walked the walk. He first burst on the scene in 1991 with a come-from-behind knockout of Michael Nunn that gave him his first world title at middleweight.

What followed were consistent meetings with the best in the business: Reggie Johnson, Mike McCallum, Iran Barkley, Roy Jones Jr., and Montell Griffin. There were hiccups along the way, when weight or a lack of focus hurt Toney on fight night, but when he was on, he was a scary, defensive wizard who could make you miss and then make you pay.

Remarkably, Toney took his old-school skill set up with him as he changed weight classes, most notably in two big fights: when he defeated Vassiliy Jirov in an epic 2003 bout that earned him a cruiserweight world title, and in a ninth-round TKO of Evander Holyfield less than six months later that put him in line for a heavyweight title fight.

In 2005, Toney got that title fight against John Ruiz, but his victory was overturned to a no contest and his championship was stripped when he tested positive for steroids. Undeterred, Toney competed for another twelve years. He didn't get that heavyweight crown, but on the nights when everything clicked, he was still a wonder to watch.

FÉLIX TRINIDAD

★★★★★ "TITO" ★★★★★

CUPEY ALTO, PUERTO RICO
BORN: January 10, 1973
HEIGHT: 5'11"
RECORD: 42–3 (35 KOs)
TITLES WON: World Champion at Welterweight, Junior Middleweight, and Middleweight
HALL OF FAME INDUCTION: 2014

Sometimes it's hard to find the joy in boxing, and that's understandable. It's often a sport that doesn't treat its athletes well, in or out of the ring.

That's why we always needed Félix Trinidad.

In early 2004, the fighting pride of Cupey Alto, Puerto Rico (already an established star at home and around the globe) was in Madison Square Garden to announce his comeback fight against Ricardo Mayorga after a two-year absence.

As Trinidad made his way to his car after the press conference, he was mobbed by fans. I managed to get close to "Tito" and asked him what he missed the most during his layoff.

He smiled his megawatt smile and started slapping himself in the face.

"I missed the punches," said Trinidad. And he meant it. Simply put, he loved the game. You could see it in his face as soon as he was introduced on fight night, when he mouthed his own name in unison with the ring announcer.

Of course, when the bell rang, the three-division world champion was a killer with a potent left hook and the ability to land it seemingly at will. But the joy was still evident as he chopped down the best of the 1990s into the new millennium. Héctor Camacho, Yori Boy Campas, Oba Carr, Pernell Whitaker, Oscar De La Hoya, David Reid, Fernando Vargas, William Joppy, and Mayorga all dotted his resume. And although he was perhaps Puerto Rico's greatest boxer, what made "Tito" special was how he made everyone feel, which was evident when he fell for the first time against Bernard Hopkins.

It was two weeks after 9/11 in New York City, and I was taking the train after the fight. Two Trinidad fans, draped in Puerto Rican flags, sat at the end of the car and cried. Their hero had lost.

KOSTYA TSZYU

 "THUNDER FROM DOWN UNDER"

SYDNEY, AUSTRALIA
BORN: September 19, 1969
HEIGHT: 5'7"
RECORD: 31–2, 1 NC (25 KOs)
TITLES WON: World Junior Welterweight Champion
HALL OF FAME INDUCTION: 2011

Kostya Tszyu was a serious man—so serious that, at just five-foot-seven and 140 pounds, he struck an intimidating figure wherever he went. This was true even in press conferences.

Tszyu, already three years into his second reign as junior welterweight champion, sat around a table with reporters days before his title defense against Oktay Urkal in June 2021. He was polite but stone faced, moving a set of worry beads through his fingers as he spoke. The subject of his two sons, six-year-old Timofei and two-year-old Nikita, came up.

"I try to tell them that this is no joke," Tszyu said. "When you come to the gym, it's serious. They're living different lives than I am. I was hungrier than they are now. And to be successful in boxing, you have to be hungry . . . I don't want things to be easy for him. It's a beginning. If it toughens him, he's richer."

Today Tim Tszyu is a former world champion and one of the best 154-pound boxers in the world. Nikita is an unbeaten prospect with championship potential. As for their dad, he was one of the best junior welterweights in the history of the division, a wrecking machine who proudly represented his native Russia and adopted country of Australia, and a boxer who sent shivers down the spine of 140-pound fighters from 1992 to 2005.

During a career like that, it's easy to dismiss the first several years, simply because it's usually a developmental time filled with bouts against opponents designed to push, but not push too hard.

That wasn't the case with Tszyu, a decorated amateur who had the names of former world champion Juan La Porte and Livingstone Bramble on his victims list within ten pro fights. In his fourteenth fight, he stopped Jake Rodríguez in the sixth round to win the IBF super welterweight title. Except for an upset loss to Vince Phillips in 1997, he was unstoppable.

Roger Mayweather, Rafael Ruelas, Miguel Ángel González, Julio César Chávez, Sharmba Mitchell, Zab Judah, and Jesse James Leija were all defeated by the "Thunder from Down Under." Only Ricky Hatton stopped the reign for good, halting Tszyu in eleven rounds in June 2005.

Tszyu retired after the bout. Six years later, he was in the International Boxing Hall of Fame, free to watch his sons create their own legacies in the fight game.

GENE TUNNEY

 "THE FIGHTING MARINE"

NEW YORK, NY
BORN: May 25, 1897
DIED: November 7, 1978
HEIGHT: 6'0"
RECORD: 65–1–1 (48 KOs)
TITLES WON: World Heavyweight Champion and American Light Heavyweight Champion
HALL OF FAME INDUCTION: 1990

Gene Tunney wasn't like the other boxers of his day—or any day, for that matter. A veteran of World Wars I and II, "The Fighting Marine" was the well-read thinking man's fighter who preferred to outsmart his foes instead of outbrawl them.

Yet don't think for a moment that Tunney was afraid of a good ol' fashioned scrap. He got in there with a who's who of the sport during his time in the ring. When that time was up, Tunney left with a 65–1–1 record and championships in the heavyweight and light heavyweight divisions; when the International Boxing Hall of Fame was created in 1990, he was part of the inaugural class.

Tunney is best remembered for his two championship fights with Jack Dempsey, both of which he won via unanimous decision. In the first, he won the heavyweight title in Philadelphia in 1926. In the 1927 rematch, he successfully defended his crown, even though he had to rise off the canvas to do so. And when he hit the deck in the seventh round, what followed was one of the most debated moments in boxing history, known as "The Long Count." Many feel that Tunney had more than ten seconds to get to his feet because Dempsey didn't follow the rule of going to a neutral corner after the knockdown, but Tunney insisted that he had his wits about him and would have made it to his feet whenever he wanted to. Regardless, Tunney rose before the count of ten and went on to win another decision.

He defended his title once more against Tom Heeney before retiring. His reign as heavyweight champion is the first thing on many fans' minds when it comes to the erudite New Yorker, but he may have

done his best work at light heavyweight, where he defeated Battling Levinsky, Tommy Loughran, Jimmy Delaney, and Georges Carpentier. He also fought Harry Greb five times. This classic pentalogy saw Tunney suffer the only loss of his pro career, in their first bout. But the thinker was always willing to study and learn: Tunney returned for two wins, one draw, and one no contest against his fellow hall-of-famer.

MIKE TYSON

★★★★★ "IRON MIKE" ★★★★★

BROOKLYN, NY
BORN: June 30, 1966
HEIGHT: 5'10"
RECORD: 50–7, 2 NC (44 KOs)
TITLES WON: Two-Time World Heavyweight Champion
HALL OF FAME INDUCTION: 2011

For those of a certain age, Mike Tyson *was* boxing. With an aggressive style, immense knockout power, and the charisma to captivate any room upon arrival, Tyson was the fighter who saved the sport in the years after Muhammad Ali and Sugar Ray Leonard ruled it. But why him and not any of the other boxers who excelled in the '80s and '90s?

"I don't know why, I have no idea," Tyson told me. "I really couldn't tell you. I wish I could."

Start with his story. Born and raised in Brownsville, Brooklyn, Tyson was a troubled youth who ultimately wound up in a reform school, where he would find boxing through a counselor and former pro fighter, Bobby Stewart. Stewart, noticing Tyson's raw talent, introduced him to Cus D'Amato, trainer and manager to the likes of Floyd Patterson and José Torres.

That's where it began. Fans and the media fell in love with the story of Cus and the Kid, and with managers Jimmy Jacobs and Bill Cayton coming in later to push the story, the Tyson era began.

And while it was Tyson's era through and through, there would be ups and downs, beginning with Tyson getting into trouble outside of the ring and D'Amato dying in 1985. The world's fascination with "Kid Dynamite" didn't wane, though, especially not after he won the world heavyweight title at twenty years old with a second-round TKO of Trevor Berbick in November of 1986.

Tyson, whose first reign was highlighted by a 91-second knockout of Michael Spinks, lost his title to Buster Douglas in 1990, in perhaps the greatest boxing upset of all time.

The defeat marked the beginning of a decline of Tyson, who served three years in prison for rape, a conviction he still protests to this day. Upon his return to the ring, he quickly regained the heavyweight title but then lost it to Evander Holyfield. In their 1997 rematch, Tyson famously bit Holyfield's ear, earning him a suspension from the ring. He would fight ten

times before retiring in 2005 and even made a 2024 comeback at fifty-seven years old to face Jake Paul.

Through it all, Tyson remains beloved by his legion of fans and is a pop culture icon revered by millions. As for how they will remember him, Tyson says, "I would like to hope that when they do mention my name ... I don't want to have to be the greatest fighter. I want them to say that [he] was the meanest, the most ferocious and vicious fighter the world has ever known, and [they'll] never see his kind again."

OLEKSANDR USYK

★★★★★ "THE CAT" ★★★★★

SIMFEROPOL, CRIMEA, UKRAINE
BORN: January 17, 1987
HEIGHT: 6'3"
RECORD: 23–0 (14 KOs)*
TITLES WON: World Heavyweight and Cruiserweight Champion; 2012 Olympic Gold Medalist

*As of press date

If you didn't know that Oleksandr Usyk was an elite boxer and world champion, you might confuse him for a comedian or dancer. But don't let the gap-toothed smile fool you.

"If I am smiling, if I am laughing, that's a true laugh and a true smile," he said. "If I need to be serious, I am serious because I have to be serious at that point. Since I was a kid, I always was happy, I always was joking. I like jokes, I like comedy movies, I like to talk to people, and I just want to be myself. If I'm going to go to the fight, I am serious and I put my mind into it. If I need to be aggressive, I'll be aggressive. But the most important thing for me is to be myself."

Being himself has worked out pretty well for the Ukrainian, an Olympic gold medalist in the 2012 Games who retired from the amateur ranks with a 335-15 record. That remarkable slate meant that when Usyk entered the pro game in 2013, he was going to be moved fast.

That was fine with the southpaw, who won his first world title at cruiserweight in just his tenth pro fight when he decisioned Krzysztof Głowacki in September of 2016. Within a year, the boxer-puncher with immaculate technique and an iron chin was seeking to unify all the belts in the division, and if that didn't take place, he teased a move to heavyweight.

"If it's not gonna happen, it's not gonna happen," he said of cruiserweight unification. "I'm not going to be just waiting for someone to come here. I'll move to the heavyweight division."

Usyk got his wish, winning all the cruiserweight belts by defeating Murat Gassiev in July of 2018. But, ultimately, that wasn't enough for his ambitious soul, as he did move up to heavyweight, where he has already defeated Anthony Joshua (twice), Daniel Dubois, and Tyson Fury (twice), becoming the first undisputed heavyweight champion in nearly a quarter of a century.

Now that's a reason to smile.

MICKEY WALKER

 "THE TOY BULLDOG"

ELIZABETH, NY
BORN: July 13, 1901
DIED: April 28, 1981
HEIGHT: 5'7"
RECORD: 93–19–4, 2 NC (59 KOs)
TITLES WON: World Champion at Middleweight and Welterweight
HALL OF FAME INDUCTION: 1990

The heavyweight division has always been in the spotlight, which isn't surprising, considering some of the outsize personalities that have held the championship belt, from John L. Sullivan to Muhammad Ali to Mike Tyson. So seeing five-foot-seven Mickey Walker steal the spotlight from the big boys made it clear that the charismatic and talented "Toy Bulldog" was something special.

Charismatic outside the ring and a killer between the ropes, Walker was a staple among the elite, at 147 and 160 pounds, where he won two divisional titles and produced a hall-of-fame career.

But what truly captivated fans throughout his sixteen-year career wasn't that he just won fights: It was that he won them with his aggressive, two-fisted style against the baddest of the bad. In one of the most talent-rich eras in boxing history, Walker defeated Jack Britton, Lew Tendler, Mike McTigue, and Tiger Flowers, to name a few; he also stepped into the ring with Harry Greb and Tommy Loughran. And when the mood struck, he took himself up to the heavyweight division, drawing with Jack Sharkey and taking on Paulino Uzcudun and Max Schmeling.

Walker never got a title shot at heavyweight, but frankly, he didn't need it for his resume. Everything he did at welterweight and middleweight (and, later, light heavyweight) was enough. The New Jersey native retired in 1935 with ninety-three wins and fifty-nine knockouts to his name. He also went on to earn acclaim for his work as an artist.

ANDRE WARD

 "S.O.G."

OAKLAND, CA
BORN: February 23, 1984
HEIGHT: 6'0"
RECORD: 32–0 (16 KOs)
TITLES WON: World Champion at Super Middleweight and Light Heavyweight; 2004 Olympic Gold Medalist
HALL OF FAME INDUCTION: 2021

In a life filled with memorable quotes, one of Muhammad Ali's best was: "I am the greatest. I said that even before I knew I was. I figured that if I said it enough, I would convince the world that I was really the greatest."

Andre Ward never talked about his greatness, even though he was a modern-era star who became the last American to win an Olympic gold medal in boxing in 2004 and then went on to dominate the super middleweight and light heavyweight divisions as a pro. The way the Oakland native saw it, that was for other people to decide.

"I feel like greatness is something that the fans give you, something that the media gives you collectively, and I just don't think it's something that, because you've had a few good battles, you can say that you're the greatest. I don't think it's something you can crown yourself with."

Ward did things his own way. He even titled his 2023 memoir *Killing the Image*. Perhaps that was the reason he was one of the best: because he didn't conform. Interviews with Ward went into directions far removed from the usual soundbites. In the ring, he also strayed from the conventional, doing whatever it took for him to get his hand raised.

There were still skeptics, though, even after Ward began taking out big name after big name at 168 pounds. But when he won the Super Six World Boxing Classic tournament, defeating Mikkel Kessler, Allan Green, Arthur Abraham, and Carl Froch, the doubters disappeared.

But the fighter dubbed S.O.G. (Son of God) wasn't satisfied. He moved up to the light heavyweight division and won and defended the title in a two-fight series with Russian knockout artist Sergey Kovalev. Following the second Kovalev bout, which he won via eighth-round TKO, Ward announced his retirement on September 21, 2017, at the age of thirty-three.

His final record? A perfect 32–0, with sixteen knockouts.

PERNELL WHITAKER

 "SWEET PEA"

NORFOLK, VA
BORN: January 2, 1964
DIED: July 14, 2019
HEIGHT: 5'6"
RECORD: 40–4–1, 1 NC (17 KOs)
TITLES WON: World Champion at Lightweight, Junior Welterweight, Welterweight, and Junior Middleweight; 1984 Olympic Gold Medalist
HALL OF FAME INDUCTION: 2006

Look up most boxers' highlight reels on the Internet, and you'll see an array of jaw-dropping knockouts and toe-to-toe slugfests. Search for Pernell Whitaker, and you'll find some of the best defensive boxing ever witnessed in the squared circle.

That's rare. Although Whitaker was appreciated during his era in the ring, he was finally starting to get his just due from a new generation in the years before his untimely death in 2019 at the age of fifty-five.

"I've been getting more appreciated since retirement," Whitaker told me in one of his last interviews. "I get more acknowledgment now than I did when I was fighting. That's great, and I appreciate it because I see it every day. Every place I go, they recognize and acknowledge that nobody did it better than Pernell Whitaker—nobody."

Sure, the Norfolk, Virginia, native is bragging a bit, but he's not far off the mark. A chess master in a sport where most are playing checkers, Whitaker was special from the jump. After winning Olympic gold for the United States in 1984, he hit the ground running in the pro ranks, dazzling foes who couldn't figure out this puzzle known as "Sweet Pea."

Unfortunately, many judges couldn't figure out Whitaker, either, and that resulted in him losing his first world title shot to José Luis Ramírez in 1988, which was widely considered to be one of the worst decisions in boxing history. Whitaker got his lightweight title a year later by beating Greg Haugen, and he avenged his loss to Ramírez, but the judges reared their ugly head again in his 1993 SuperFight with Julio César Chávez. That bout was ruled a draw,

with *Sports Illustrated* putting the fight on the cover with the headline, "Robbery."

"There's one thing about controversy," said Whitaker. "Controversy always sells. The world watched it, and I can live with going into a supermarket and they still talk about it. It's still a big thing to a lot of people, and that was a highway robbery. It was worth being on the cover of *Sports Illustrated*."

The fans knew the real story of that fight, and so did the boxing business, which continued to put Whitaker in big fights against the likes of Oscar De La Hoya (another questionable decision) and Félix Trinidad. And although his defense was his calling card, Whitaker insisted that he brought more to the ring than being able to make opponents miss. He could make them pay, too.

"I know they love the defense, but the offense I had was beautiful," said Whitaker, who retired in 2001 and was inducted into the International Boxing Hall of Fame in his first year of eligibility, in 2006. "Some of the guys, I knew I could have probably got them out of there, but they just get on your nerves, so I just like to drag 'em all twelve rounds and just punish 'em along the way."

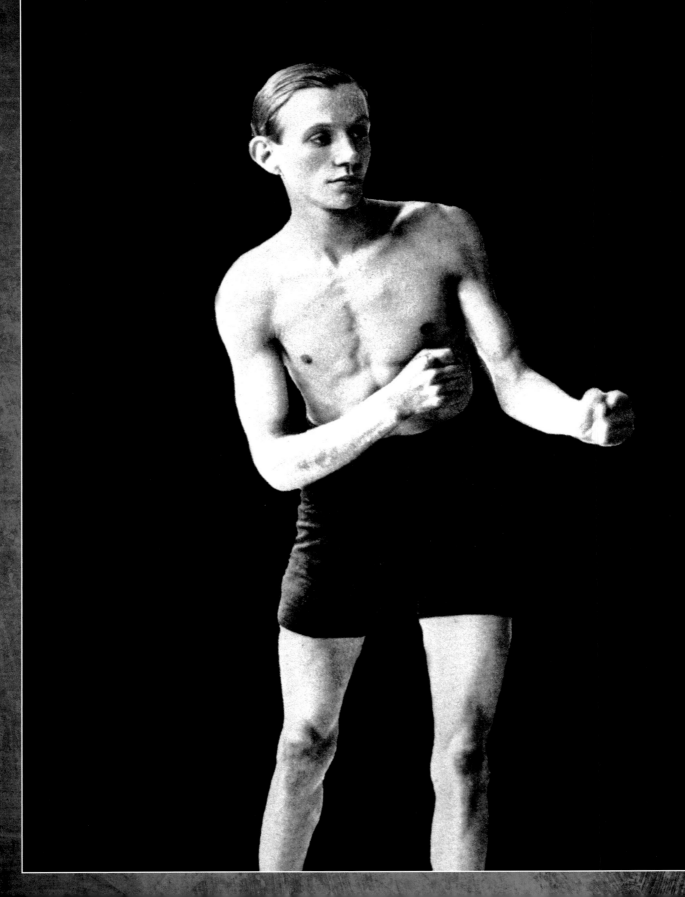

JIMMY WILDE

 **"THE MIGHTY ATOM"**

TYLORSTOWN, WALES
BORN: May 15, 1892
DIED: March 10, 1969
HEIGHT: 5'2½"
RECORD: 131–3–1, 21 NC (98 KOs)
TITLES WON: World Flyweight Champion
HALL OF FAME INDUCTION: 1990

Poor Jimmy Wilde. That had to be the opinion of anyone who saw the Welshman on weigh-in day or when he stepped into the ring on fight night.

Simply put, he looked like a stiff wind would knock him over. But then the bell rang, and 131 times from 1911 to 1923, Wilde had his hand raised. And ninety-eight times, the judges didn't need to get involved. That 75 percent knockout rate is impressive in any weight class in any era. But for a 112-pound flyweight to be shutting lights out like that was unheard of.

Today Wilde, a member of the International Boxing Hall of Fame's inaugural 1990 class, is considered by more than a few people to be the best British boxer of all time. Some even call him the best ever, regardless of weight class.

That's high praise for someone who weighed just seventy-four pounds when he began boxing as a teenager. Wilde eventually grew into his five-foot-two-and-a-half-inch frame and dominated in the newly instituted flyweight division. He went 94–0–1 before suffering his first loss in 1915 to Tancy Lee, who outweighed him by at least fourteen pounds. Wilde avenged the defeat by knockout a year later. A week before Christmas 1916, he halted Young Zulu Kid in the eleventh round to become the first flyweight world champion.

Legacy set. Wilde retired after two defeats to Pete Herman and Pancho Villa, making it clear that the only way to keep "The Mighty Atom" down was through the intervention of Father Time.

IKE WILLIAMS

BRUNSWICK, GA
BORN: August 2, 1923
DIED: September 5, 1994
HEIGHT: 5'9"
RECORD: 126–24–4 (61 KOs)
TITLES WON: World Lightweight Champion
HALL OF FAME INDUCTION: 1990

Most people are trying to figure out life at 21 years old. Ike Williams went into Mexico City at twenty-one and stopped hometown hero Juan Zurita in two rounds to win the lightweight championship of the world.

That's called growing up fast. The Georgia native had no problem with that part of the gig, even at El Toreo de Cuatro Caminos, where Zurita's fans crowded the ring, requiring a police escort to get Williams back to the locker room.

By that time, the rest of the boxing universe already knew who the potent punching Williams was. With seventy-three fights already under his belt by the time he was crowned champion, Williams had practically seen and done it all. But the best was yet to come for the man who held the 135-pound title for more than six years.

During his reign, Williams thrilled fans with a dominant stoppage of Bob Montgomery, avenging one of his most bitter defeats. He also turned back the likes of Kid Gavilán and Beau Jack, whom he battled four times before the two retired after their 1955 bout in Augusta, Georgia.

Many believe that Williams didn't receive the acclaim he deserved because he didn't play ball with the mob, which largely ran boxing in the 1950s. Williams was a man of pride and integrity, though, and he even testified before Congress in 1961 about his experiences in the boxing business.

Williams died of natural causes in 1994 at the age of seventy-one. Thankfully, he was able to enjoy recognition as an all-time great with his induction into the first class of the International Boxing Hall of Fame in 1990.

CARLOS ZÁRATE

 "CANAS"

MEXICO CITY, MEXICO
BORN: May 23, 1951
HEIGHT: 5'8"
RECORD: 66–4 (63 KOs)
TITLES WON: World Bantamweight Champion
HALL OF FAME INDUCTION: 1994

The punching power of Carlos Zárate can rightfully be called legendary, considering that he earned his place in the International Boxing Hall of Fame for sixty-three knockouts in sixty-six wins and three years as bantamweight champion.

They should have seen it coming: The Mexico City native ended thirty of his thirty-three wins as an amateur by knockout. A 91 percent finishing rate in the amateur ranks, with fewer rounds and more of a point-fighting style, is exceedingly rare. It really should have been an obvious warning sign to all who were going to face "Canas" after he turned pro in 1970.

Then again, all the warnings in the world weren't going to help opponents once the bell rang. In fact, Zárate didn't go the distance in a professional ring until he decisioned Víctor Ramírez over ten rounds in his twenty-fourth fight.

The knockout streak picked right back up less than a month later. This time, Zárate won twenty-eight in a row before the judges got involved. Over the course of that run, he became a popular attraction at the Forum in Inglewood, California and won the WBC bantamweight title with an eighth-round stoppage of Rodolfo Martínez in 1976.

During Zárate's reign, the boxing world demanded a showdown between him and fellow knockout artist (and WBA champion) Alfonso Zamora. In April 1977, "The Battle of the Z Boys" happened, with Zárate winning a wild bout in the fourth round.

Zárate's knockout—and winning—streak ended on October 28, 1978, at the fiery fists of Wilfredo Gómez in a championship bout up a division at 122 pounds. He successfully defended his bantamweight crown once more before he lost it in a controversial decision to Lupe Pintor that prompted him to announce his retirement.

Greatest Fights

1971
MUHAMMAD ALI vs. JOE FRAZIER I

Called "The Fight of the Century," the first meeting between unbeatens Muhammad Ali and Joe Frazier lived up to its billing at Madison Square Garden in New York City. With the world put on hold while the combatants threw hands, Frazier and Ali went back and forth for fifteen rounds, with "Smokin' Joe" parlaying a last-round knockdown to a unanimous decision victory.

1975
MUHAMMAD ALI vs. JOE FRAZIER III

No one was expecting much from the third fight between Muhammad Ali and Joe Frazier. Unlike in their first meeting in 1971, both were past their prime and had seen better days. But as the old adage goes, every great fighter has one great fight left in them. In the stifling heat in the Philippines, "The Thrilla in Manila" was just that—a brutal back-and-forth battle won by Ali when Frazier's corner threw in the towel before the fifteenth round.

1980
ROBERTO DURÁN vs. SUGAR RAY LEONARD I

It's safe to say that there was some bad blood between Roberto Durán and Sugar Ray Leonard before their first fight in 1980. Then again, Durán had bad blood with everybody, and it fueled him into a furious frenzy as he stepped into the ring in Montreal. Leonard, looking to prove a point, stood in the pocket and battled for fifteen rounds, clearly fighting Durán's fight. Although Durán got the decision, Leonard got his respect.

1981
SUGAR RAY LEONARD vs. THOMAS HEARNS I

"You're blowing it, son." Those words from trainer Angelo Dundee to his fighter, Sugar Ray Leonard, will never be forgotten. Leonard took them to heart as he came out for the thirteenth round, down on all three scorecards and in need of a knockout to win. Leonard got his knockout in the fourteenth, breaking the heart of Hearns, who had fought nearly flawlessly up until the stoppage.

1982
AARON PRYOR vs. ALEXIS ARGÜELLO I

I can't think of a better way to describe the first SuperFight between Aaron Pryor and Alexis Argüello than to simply call it violent. It seemed like every punch was thrown with bad intentions, and most of them landed. Both combatants showed their toughness throughout the contest, which finally ended with a barrage of blows from Pryor in the fourteenth round that forced a referee stoppage.

1985
MARVELOUS MARVIN HAGLER vs. THOMAS HEARNS

Today people call this fight "The War." And to think, when Marvelous Marvin Hagler and Thomas Hearns got together at Caesars Palace in Las Vegas, the fight lasted only seven minutes and fifty-two seconds. But what a time it was. Hearns came out throwing bombs, Hagler responded, and the brawl was on. The action was intense from the start. But when Hagler was cut and the bout was in danger of being stopped, he found another gear and put it on Hearns until he got the finish in the third round.

2002
MICKY WARD vs. ARTURO GATTI I

Micky Ward was a good fighter. When he met Arturo Gatti in 2002, it was expected to be a good action fight until Gatti pulled away and won it. Well, it turned out to be a *great* action fight, and Ward wasn't denied in the biggest moment of his career. He scored a ninth-round knockdown of Gatti, and although "Thunder" staged a hellacious comeback, "Irish Micky" won a majority decision that kicked off an epic trilogy between the two rivals. (They later became good friends.)

2004
MARCO ANTONIO BARRERA vs. ERIK MORALES III

A lot had changed since the first fight between Marco Antonio Barrera and Erik Morales in 2000 and the third one in 2004. Neither was a hungry kid trying to make his way in the boxing world anymore. Both were established stars, with all that comes with the status. One thing hadn't changed, though. They still didn't like each other, and they fought like bitter enemies in what many consider to be the best fight of their trilogy. With his majority decision win, Barrera took the series two fights to one.

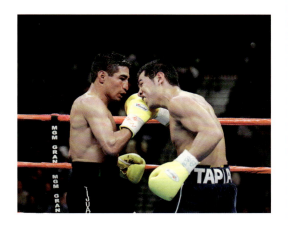

2005
DIEGO CORRALES vs. JOSÉ LUIS CASTILLO I

This was the best fight I've ever seen. Yes, it's cool to see an all-out brawl, but sometimes those fights are contested at a lower level than elite. Not this one. When Diego Corrales and José Luis Castillo clashed, it was all-out war at the highest level possible. Corrales was dropped twice in the tenth round, and somehow the drama then kicked into overdrive. Corrales took instructions from trainer Joe Goossen to heart and knocked out Castillo later in that fateful tenth frame.

2022
KATIE TAYLOR vs. AMANDA SERRANO I

You can argue for any of the earlier fights as the greatest of all time, but when it comes to women's boxing, there's no argument. The 2022 bout between Katie Taylor and Amanda Serrano was the best ever. From the atmosphere at Madison Square Garden, to the high stakes involved, to the nonstop punching round after round and the drama when the final verdict was read, these ladies ticked all the boxes of an epic fight. And it was so good that they ran it back in late 2024, with Taylor winning another action-packed (and razor-thin) decision over her Puerto Rican foe.

Greatest Knockouts

1938
JOE LOUIS vs. MAX SCHMELING II

Joe Louis was usually a patient sort, stalking his opponents while looking for the opening that would end the fight. That wasn't the case in his rematch with Max Schmeling. With World War II looming and everyone around the globe listening to the fight on the radio, Louis had business to take care of, and he wanted it done as soon as possible. At 2:04 of the first round, the match was over.

1952
ROCKY MARCIANO vs. JERSEY JOE WALCOTT I

The image is perhaps the most famous one in boxing history: Rocky Marciano catching Jersey Joe Walcott with the single right hand that ended his reign as heavyweight champion. It was a devastating blow by Marciano—and one he needed because he was down on all scorecards heading into that decisive thirteenth round. One punch, and the sport had a new king.

1957
SUGAR RAY ROBINSON vs. GENE FULLMER II

Sugar Ray Robinson was the perfect fighting machine. On May 1, 1957, he planted the perfect left hook on the chin of Gene Fullmer, ending his night in emphatic fashion. The punch itself was a thing of beauty. What made this fifth-round win even more impressive is that Robinson landed it on a fighter who had never been stopped up to that point in his career and who had gone fifteen rounds with him just three months earlier.

1980
MIKE WEAVER vs. JOHN TATE

Rising star John Tate was the WBA heavyweight champion, and he had the homefield advantage against tough contender Mike Weaver, fighting in his hometown of Knoxville, Tennessee. For fourteen rounds, Tate dominated. All he had to do was cruise through the fifteenth, and he would retain his title. Weaver had other plans. "I was waiting all night to do it," Weaver told me. "He got caught with that left hook, and he went down." Like a tree. The referee could have counted to a hundred, and it wouldn't have mattered.

1994
GEORGE FOREMAN vs. MICHAEL MOORER

The dream was about to be over for George Foreman. His comeback after ten years out of the ring made headlines around the sporting world, but the forty-five-year-old's second shot at regaining the heavyweight title wasn't going so well: Michael Moorer had been putting it on him for nine-plus rounds. But they say that the punch is the last thing to go on a fighter, and in the tenth round, "Big George" landed a right hand that put Moorer down for the count. As HBO commentator Jim Lampley exclaimed, "It happened."

2001
HASIM RAHMAN vs. LENNOX LEWIS I

I think it's safe to say that Lennox Lewis underestimated Hasim Rahman when they met for the first time in Brakpan, South Africa. And although you shouldn't do that in any weight class, it's especially dangerous for a heavyweight. In the fifth round, Rahman struck with the most important right hand of his career. Lewis fell to the canvas and was unable to rise, and a new heavyweight king was crowned.

2004
ANN WOLFE vs. VONDA WARD

Ann Wolfe was probably the biggest puncher in women's boxing history. If she caught an opponent flush, things went south for that opponent in a hurry. Vonda Ward, a six-foot-seven former basketball player, had all the physical advantages on the five-foot-ten Wolfe when they met in May 2004, but she didn't have Wolfe's punch. When the Texan got close and threw a rocket of a right hand, it detonated on Ward's chin and ended the fight immediately. Sixty-eight seconds was all it took.

2004
ANTONIO TARVER vs. ROY JONES JR. II

"You got any excuses tonight, Roy?" Those were the words Antonio Tarver spoke to Roy Jones Jr. as the referee gave them their instructions before their second fight. Their first one was close, but this time, Tarver had a chip on his shoulder, and he made it known that he was coming for blood. In round 2, he got it, stunning the boxing world with a left hand that ended Jones's night and shattered his aura of invincibility forever.

2010
SERGIO MARTÍNEZ vs. PAUL WILLIAMS

Argentina's Sergio Martínez was not known as a knockout artist, but he was a sniper. If a sniper gets a read on somebody, like Martínez did on Paul Williams in the second round of their 2010 rematch, it's lights out. That was precisely the case when Martínez nailed Williams with a perfect left cross. Williams was out on impact, and when he fell face-first to the mat, the count was academic. He wasn't getting up before the count of ten.

2012
JUAN MANUEL MÁRQUEZ vs. MANNY PACQUIAO IV

I'll be completely honest: When Juan Manuel Márquez knocked out Manny Pacquiao in their fourth fight, I thought he had killed the Filipino icon. That's how scary this knockout was, as Pacquiao ran into a flush right hand and collapsed to the canvas face-first. I'll say it again: It was scary. Thankfully, Pacquiao eventually got back to his feet and continued his career, but that was something no one needs to see again. (Or maybe you do, if you're like me and a sucker for one-punch knockouts.)

SAT PLAYOFF KNICKS \ BOSTON
SUN RANGERS \ TORONTO
MON ALL STAR WRESTLING SHOW
SAMMARTINO \GORILLA MONSOON
MAR 29 RANGERS \ DETROIT
ROUND
MAR 31 BOXING COKES \ HARRIS

Best of a Nation

UNITED KINGDOM
- Jimmy Wilde
- Joe Calzaghe
- Lennox Lewis
- Jimmy McLarnin
- Tyson Fury

USA
- Sugar Ray Robinson
- Muhammad Ali
- Joe Louis
- Sugar Ray Leonard
- Floyd Mayweather Jr.

REST OF EUROPE
- Wladimir Klitschko
- Oleksandr Usyk
- Gennadiy Golovkin
- Max Schmeling
- Vasyl Lomachenko

ASIA
- Manny Pacquiao
- Fighting Harada
- Naoya Inoue
- Khaosai Galaxy
- Nonito Donaire

AFRICA
- Azumah Nelson
- Dick Tiger
- Ike Quartey
- Vic Toweel
- John Mugabi

PUERTO RICO
- Félix Trinidad
- Wilfredo Gómez
- Wilfred Benítez
- Miguel Cotto
- Carlos Ortiz

MEXICO
- Julio César Chávez
- Salvador Sánchez
- Rubén Olivares
- Juan Manuel Márquez
- Marco Antonio Barrera

REST OF THE WORLD
- Éder Jofre
- Roberto Durán
- Alexis Argüello
- José Nápoles
- Jeff Fenech

INSIGHT
EDITIONS

PO Box 3088
San Rafael, CA 94912
www.insighteditions.com

Find us on Facebook: www.facebook.com/InsightEditions
Follow us on Instagram: @insighteditions

All rights reserved. Published by Insight Editions, San Rafael, California, in 2025.

No part of this book may be reproduced in any form without
written permission from the publisher.

IE ISBN: 979-8-88663-850-9
UK ISBN: 979-8-3374-0301-4

Publisher: Raoul Goff
SVP, Group Publisher: Vanessa Lopez
VP, Creative: Chrissy Kwasnik
VP, Manufacturing: Alix Nicholaeff
Publishing Director: Mike Degler
Executive Editor: Jennifer Sims
Assistant Editor: Alec Zapata
Editorial Assistant: Jeff Chiarelli
Managing Editor: Nora Milman
Production Associate: Tiffani Patterson
Strategic Production Planner: Lina s Palma-Temena

Thanks to Malea-Clark Nicholson for her design support and Amazing15 for the cover design.

ROOTS of PEACE   REPLANTED PAPER

Insight Editions, in association with Roots of Peace, will plant two trees for each tree
used in the manufacturing of this book. Roots of Peace is an internationally renowned humanitarian
organization dedicated to eradicating land mines worldwide and converting war-torn lands into productive
farms and wildlife habitats. Roots of Peace will plant two million fruit and nut trees in Afghanistan and provide
farmers there with the skills and support necessary for sustainable land use.

Manufactured in China by Insight Editions

10 9 8 7 6 5 4 3 2 1

---

via Getty Images:
Pages 4, 21, 131: Al Bello/Hulton Archive, Pages 6, 46, 56, 75, 83-85, 87, 99, 110, 123, 193, 209: Focus on Sport/Getty Images Sport, Pages 8, 18, 38, 100, 115, 124, 199, 204: The Stanley Weston Archive/Archive Photos, Pages 10-11, 14, 25, 36, 42, 52, 54, 64, 69-71, 73, 80, 92, 94, 97, 108, 118, 126, 134, 136, 140, 148, 151, 157, 165, 168, 172, 174, 180, 182, 184, 190, 200, 214, 216-217, 222: Bettmann/Bettmann, Pages 12, 176, 219: Sarah Stier/Getty Images Sport, Pages 17, 218: George Tiedemann/Sports Illustrated, Page 22: Hy Peskin Archive/Archive Photos, Page 26: Charles Del Vecchio/The Washington Post, Page 29: Cris Esqueda (Golden Boy)/Getty Images Sport, Page 30: Charles "Teenie" Harris/Carnegie Museum of Art, Page 32: John Gichigi/Getty Images Sport, Page 34: The Asahi Shimbun/The Asahi Shimbun, Pages 40, 57, 187: Holly Stein/Getty Images Sport, Pages 44, 62, 66, 113, 116, 130, 160, 219: Al Bello/Getty Images Sport, Page 48: American Stock Archive/Archive Photos, Page 51: Manny Millan/Sports Illustrated, Page 58: Herb Scharfman (Sports Imagery)/Getty Images Sport, Page 61: Dick Morseman (Newsday LLC)/Newsday, Page 76: Danny Gohlke/Bongarts, Page 77: TORSTEN SILZ/DDP (AFP), Page 78: Tom Pidgeon/Hulton Archive, Pages 88, 128: Jed Jacobsohn/Getty Images Sport, Page 89: Tom Briglia/WireImage, Page 90: Paul Devlin (SNS Group)/SNS Group, Page 96: PhotoQuest/Archive Photos, Page 102: Alexander Hassenstein/Bongarts, Page 104: AFP/AFP, Page 106: Topical Press Agency/Hulton Archive, Pages 111, 201: Focus on Sport/Focus on Sport, Page 112: Jed Jacobsohn/Hulton Archive, Page 121: Keystone-France/Gamma-Keystone, Page 127: Hulton Deutsch/Corbis Historical, Page 132: Ethan Miller/Getty Images Sport, Page 138: El Grafico/Getty Images Sport, Page 143: Vince Bucci/AFP, Page 144: Craig Durling/WireImage, Page 146: Ker Lavine/Getty Images Sport, Page 152: Central Press/Hulton Archive, Pages 154, 206: Christian Petersen/Getty Images Sport, Page 158: Anthony Barboza/Archive Photos, Page 162: Al Fenn/The Chronicle Collection, Page 164: Underwood Archives/Archive Photos, Page 166: Chicago History Museum/Archive Photos Page 170: James Drake/Sports Illustrated, Page 178: Gregory Shamus/Getty Images Sport, Page 181: Bob Riha, Jr./Archive Photos, Page 188: Bill Tompkins/Michael Ochs Archives, Page 194: TIMOTHY A. CLARY/AFP, Page 196: Eliot J. Schechter/Getty Images Sport, Page 197: Nick Potts (PA Images)/PA Images, Page 202: Francois Nel/Getty Images Sport, Page 210: S&G (PA Images)/PA Image Archive, Page 212: Keystone (Stringer)/Hulton Archive, Page 220: JOHN GURZINSKI (Stringer)/AFP, Page 221: Robert Beck/Sports Illustrated

via Library of Congress:
Page 149: Bain News Service/George Grantham Bain Collection

LAILA ALI, **MUHAMMAD ALI**, Saúl Álvarez, Lo Marco Antonio Barrera, Carmen Basilio, Wilfre Burley, Joe Calzaghe, Miguel Canto, Tony Ca Conn, Terrence Crawford, **OSCAR DE LA HOYA GEORGE FOREMAN**, Bob Foster, **JOE FRAZI** Gómez, Harry Greb, Emile Griffith, Marvin H Harada, Thomas Hearns, Larry Holmes, **EVAN** Éder Jofre, **JACK JOHNSON**, Roy Jones Jr., S Sam Langford, Benny Leonard, **SUGAR RAY LEC** Tommy Loughran, Joe Louis, Ray Mancini, R Martin, **FLOYD MAYWEATHER JR.**, Terry Mc Moore, Erik Morales, Shane Mosley, Azumah N **MANNY PACQUIAO**, Willie Pep, Aaron Pryor, L Tommy Ryan, Matthew Saad Muhammad, Sa Claressa Shields, Michael Spinks, Young Strib Dick Tiger, James Toney, Felix Trinidad, Kost Usyk, Mickey Walker, Andre Ward, Pernell W